Mark Foley   Diane Hall

ELEMENTARY

Total English

Students' Book

PEARSON
Longman

Contents

LESSON 3	COMMUNICATION	FILM BANK
Grammar: *a/an;* negative forms of *to be* **Vocabulary:** jobs **Can do:** understand and complete a simple form	**Can do:** start and finish a basic conversation	Meeting people **page 131**
Grammar: *this, that, these, those,* noun plurals **Vocabulary:** everyday objects; colours; some adjectives **Can do:** identify everyday objects	**Can do:** ask simple questions for information and understand simple answers	Unreal City **page 132**
Functions: making suggestions; using the phone **Vocabulary:** large numbers **Can do:** understand and leave a simple phone message	**Can do:** talk about other people's abilities	Deborah's day **page 133**
Grammar: object pronouns; *I'd like* **Vocabulary:** menus, prices **Can do:** order food in a fast food restaurant	**Can do:** shop for food at a market	Two soups **page 134**
Grammar: modifiers *(very, quite, really)* **Vocabulary:** adjectives to describe places **Can do:** write an informal email about your country	**Can do:** talk about furnishing an apartment	ResidenSea **page 135**
Grammar: Past Simple: negative **Vocabulary:** transport **Can do:** describe your last holiday	**Can do:** understand a store guide and ask for things in shops	Amazing buildings **page 136**
Grammar: Past Simple: irregular verbs **Vocabulary:** phrasal verbs **Can do:** understand an article	**Can do:** identify a person from a simple description	Great Expectations **page 137**
Grammar: Present Simple and Present Continuous **Vocabulary:** the weather; health **Can do:** take part in a factual conversation on a simple topic	**Can do:** make a complaint in a shop, write a simple letter of complaint	The Notting Hill Carnival **page 138**
Grammar: *prefer* + noun/*-ing* form; *will* for spontaneous decisions and offers **Vocabulary:** art **Can do:** talk about personal preferences	**Can do:** discuss and plan activities	Spirit of the city **page 139**
Grammar: *-ing* form as a noun (subject only) **Vocabulary:** types of transport **Can do:** book a travel ticket	**Can do:** understand basic hotel information, book a hotel room	Commuting **page 140**
Grammar: Present Continuous for future **Vocabulary:** education **Can do:** talk about future arrangements	**Can do:** make future arrangements and appointments	Rock climbing **page 141**
Grammar: verbs + infinitive/*-ing* form *(want, would like, like,* etc.) **Vocabulary:** leisure activities **Can do:** talk about likes, dislikes and ambitions	**Can do:** plan study objectives	Ten great adventures **page 142**

Do you know...?

1 a 🔊 0.1 Do you know the alphabet? Listen and repeat the alphabet.

**a b c d e f g h i
j k l m n o p q r
s t u v w x y z**

b Listen to the alphabet again. Write the letters in the correct place.

sounds	letters
/eɪ/	a h __ __
/iː/	b c d __ __ __ __ __
/e/	f l m __ __ __ __
/aɪ/	i __
/əʊ/	o
/uː/	q __ __
/ɑː/	r

c 🔊 0.2 Listen and check your answers.

d Write six consonants and three vowels. Read them to your partner. Write your partner's list.

Consonants: _____

Vowels: _____

2 a 🔊 0.3 Do you know numbers? Match the numbers to the words. Then listen, check and repeat.

0 1 2 3 4 5 6 7 8 9 10

eight   five   four   nine   oh/zero   one
seven   six   ten   three   two

b 🔊 0.4 Complete the sequence with numbers from the box. Then listen, check and repeat.

> eighty fifty fourteen nineteen ninety seventeen seventy sixteen thirty twenty-two

11 eleven	21 twenty-one
12 twelve	22 _____
13 thirteen	30 _____
14 _____	40 forty
15 fifteen	50 _____
16 _____	60 sixty
17 _____	70 _____
18 eighteen	80 _____
19 _____	90 _____
20 twenty	100 a hundred

3 a Do you know classroom instructions? Match the instructions to the pictures.

> Complete. Ask and answer. Correct. Match. Look at page... Check your answers. Write. Repeat. Listen. Read.

b 🔊 0.5 Listen and check your answers.

4 a Do you know English words? Look at the photos. Write the things you see in the table.

FOOD / DRINK	
FAMILY	
EQUIPMENT	
SPORT	
TRANSPORT	
COLOURS	

b Work in groups. Do you know other English words? Write them in the table.

1 Your life

Lead-in

1 a **1.1** Complete the dialogues. Use expressions from the box. Then listen and check.

> My name's   Hello   Hi   What's your name   I'm   It's   meet

A

1 A: Hi _____ Jana. _____ _____ _____?
   B: _____, Jana. _____ _____ Dominik.
2 A: _____ _____ _____, please?
   B: _____ Patricia Pérez.
3 A: Hello. _____ _____ David Cooper.
   B: _____. _____ Lisa Smith. Nice to _____ you.

b Match the three dialogues to the three photos on the left.

c Practise the dialogues with your classmates.

B

2 a **1.2** Listen and repeat this phone number.

020 651 347

b **1.3** Now listen and write the phone numbers.

01452 946 713

c Practise with a partner.

A: Say a phone number from Exercise 2b.
B: Point at the correct number.

C

1.1 People and places

Grammar	subject pronouns + positive forms of *to be*
Can do	talk about where you are from

Vocabulary | countries and nationalities

1 Find the countries on the map.

United States of America A☐   Australia ☐
Britain ☐   Brazil ☐   China ☐   Finland ☐
France ☐   Germany ☐   Greece ☐   Italy ☐
Japan ☐   Poland ☐   Russia ☐   Spain ☐
Turkey ☐

2 a Look at the photos and the box. Ask and answer.

> Gong Li   Penélope Cruz   Nicole Kidman
> a Nokia phone   a Jaguar car   Will Smith
> a Gucci handbag   ~~Paulo Coelho~~
> Roman Polanski   Ralf and Michael Schumacher
> Catherine Deneuve and Gerard Depardieu

1   A: *Who is he?*   B: *He's Paulo Coelho.*

2   A: *Who is she?*   B: *She's ...*

3   A: *What is it?*   B: *It's ...*

4   A: *Who are they?*   B: *They're ...*

b Match the photos to the countries.

Paulo Coelho - Brazil

Philadelphia

Atlantic Ocean

Pacific Ocean

A

B

Río do Janeiro

3 a Ask and answer about the people and objects in the photos.

A: *Where is Paulo Coelho from?*
B: *He's from Brazil. He's Brazilian.*
A: *Where are Nokia phones from?*
B: *They're from Finland. They're Finnish.*

b 〔1.4〕 Listen and check your answers.

4 Complete the table. Then listen again and check.

COUNTRY	NATIONALITY	ENDING
Australia	1 *Australian*	*(i)an*
2 _____	American	
Brazil	3 _____	
Italy	4 _____	
5 _____	German	
Russia	Russian	
6 _____	Spanish	*ish*
Poland	7 _____	
Britain	8 _____	
9 _____	Finnish	
Turkey	Turkish	
China	10 _____	*ese*
Japan	Japanese	
11 _____	French	
Greece	Greek	

Madrid •

Shenyang •

Pacific
Ocean

Indian
Ocean

Pronunciation

5 a 🔊 1.5 Listen and repeat the nationality words.

> **Lifelong learning**
>
> How to record stress
>
> <u>Under</u>line the syllable with the strong sound.
>
> Aus<u>tra</u>lian

b Listen again. Write the words and <u>underline</u> the stress.

c Practise the words. **Student A:** say a name. **Student B:** say the nationality.

A: *Roman Polanski*

B: *He's Polish.*

6 a Where are the people from? Write the names.

I'm from Rio de Janeiro. = *Paulo Coelho*

1 I'm from Philadelphia. = _____
2 We're from Germany. = _____
3 I'm from Madrid. = _____
4 I'm from Shenyang. = _____
5 We're from France. = _____

b Imagine you are one of the people in the pictures. Who are you? Ask and answer.

A: *Where are you from?*

B: *I'm from Rio de Janeiro.*

A: *You're Paulo Coelho.*

B: *Yes, that's right.*

Grammar | *to be* (positive)

7 a Complete the Active grammar box with *am, is* or *are*.

> **Active grammar**
>
> I _____ (I'm)
> You __are__ (you're)
> He _____ (he's)
> She _____ (she's)   from
> It _____ (it's)   Russia.
> We _____ (we're)
> You _____ (you're)
> They _____ (they're)

see Reference page 13

b Complete the sentences.

I *'m* Brazilian. *I* 'm from São Paulo.

1 Jennifer López _____ American. _____'s from New York.
2 We'_____ Polish. _____'re from Warsaw.
3 A: Excuse me, where _____ you _____?
   B: I'_____ from Colombia.
4 A: What is _____? B: It'_____ a dictionary.
5 A: Who are _____? B: They'_____ students in my class.

8 Race your classmates. Work in pairs. Say the name of a country to another pair. Write names of famous people and things from the country in two minutes.

1.2 Family ties

Grammar	possessive 's; possessive adjectives; yes/no questions with to be
Can do	exchange information about your family

Vocabulary | families

1 What are their relationships? Match 1–5 to the pictures (A–E).

1 father and son ☐
2 mother and daughter ☐
3 brothers ☐
4 sisters ☐
5 husband and wife ☐

2 Match the sentence halves.

1 Julio Iglesias is   a Bill's wife.
2 Hillary Clinton is   b Serena's sister.
3 Venus Williams is   c Enrique's father.
4 Prince Harry is   d Madonna's daughter.
5 Lourdes is   e Prince William's brother.

Grammar | possessive 's

3 Choose the correct sentence.

1 Bill is Hillary husband.
2 Bill is Hillary's husband.

see Reference page 13

4 **a** This is the Bundy family from TV's *Married ... with Children*. Complete the Bundy family tree.

	=	*Peggy*

	Bud

b Make eight sentences about the family. Use 's.

> ~~wife~~   ~~son~~   husband   sister   brother
> mother   father   daughter

Peggy is Al's wife. Bud is Al and Peggy's son.

5 **a** Match the family words to the meanings.

1 mother and father   a uncle
2 sons and daughters   b grandmother
3 father's or mother's brother   c nephew
4 father's or mother's sister   d parents
5 mother's or father's mother   e aunt
6 mother's or father's father   f niece
7 brother's or sister's son   g children
8 brother's or sister's daughter   h grandfather

b Find the meanings in a dictionary.

> stepbrother   father-in-law   girlfriend
> best friend   cousins   grandparents

Pronunciation

6   **a**   **1.6** Listen to the underlined sound /ʌ/.

m<u>o</u>ther   br<u>o</u>ther

b   **1.7** Listen and repeat these family words. <u>Underline</u> the sound /ʌ/ in five words.

1 husband   2 father   3 grandmother
4 sister-in-law   5 daughter   6 cousin
7 uncle   8 nephew   9 grandson   10 niece

Grammar | possessive adjectives

7   Read about the Bundy family. Complete the Active grammar box with the <u>underlined</u> words.

Hi. Welcome to my crazy family – <u>my</u> husband Al and <u>our</u> children Bud and Kelly!

Meet the Bundy family: Al Bundy is married to Peggy, <u>his</u> beautiful wife, and Bud and Kelly are <u>their</u> children. Kelly is sixteen and <u>her</u> little brother, Bud, is thirteen. They're a crazy family!

Active grammar

Subject pronouns	Possessive adjectives
I	_____
you	your
he	_____
she	_____
we	_____
you	your
they	_____

see Reference page 13

8   Complete the gaps with possessive adjectives.

Clare is <u>our</u> sister. (we)

1 _____ teacher is English. (I)
2 Mr and Mrs Schegel are _____ parents. (they)
3 What is _____ homework? (we)
4 How old is _____ best friend? (you)
5 **A:** Are _____ grandparents from Madrid? (you)
   B: Yes, they are.
6 **A:** Are _____ sisters married? (she)
   B: No, they are single.
7 **A:** Is _____ boyfriend American? (you)
   B: No, he's Australian.
8 **A:** Is Tomas _____ brother? (he)
   B: Yes, he is.

Grammar | *to be* (questions)

9   Look at sentences 5–8 in Ex. 8 again. Complete the Active grammar box with *is* or *are*.

Active grammar

	he she it	American?	Yes,	he she it	___ .
___	we you they	American?	Yes,	we you they	___ .

see Reference page 13

Listening

10   **a**   Complete the questions and answers with *she, he, my, your, is* or *are.*

1 She's nice. Is she _____ mother?
2 She's young! How old _____ she?
3 Really? And this man, is _____ your uncle?
4 Where _____ he from?
5 The girls are beautiful. Are they _____ sisters?
6 How old _____ they?

a No. Clare's _____ sister and Liz _____ her best friend.
b Well, she _____ forty-eight.
c No, he's _____ sister's boyfriend.
d No, _____'s my mother-in-law, Jack's mother.
e Clare _____ eighteen and Liz _____ twenty-two.
f He _____ from Warsaw.

b   **1.8** Listen and match 1–6 to a–f.

Person to person

11   Write the names of five people in your family. Show them to your partner. Ask and answer.

A: *Who's Elena?*
B: *She's my aunt.*
A: *Is she your mother's sister?*
B: *No, she's my father's sister.*

Grammar	*a/an*; negative forms of *to be*
Can do	understand and complete a simple form

A

B

C

D

E

F

G

H

I

Vocabulary | jobs

1 **a** Look at the photos and choose the correct words. Talk to a partner.

> an architect   an artist
> a bank clerk   a dentist
> a doctor   an electrician
> an engineer   a teacher
> a journalist   a judge
> a lawyer   a nurse
> a police officer
> a secretary
> a housewife/husband
> a shop assistant
> a student   a traffic warden
> a computer programmer
> retired   unemployed

A: *A is a secretary.*
B: *No, I think she's a journalist.*
A: *H is unemployed.*
B: *Yes, that's right.*

b Write the correct jobs.

Grammar | *a/an*

2 Look at the jobs in Ex. 1a again. Complete the Active grammar box with *a* or *an*.

> **Active grammar**
> ___
> Use _____ before vowel sounds (a, e, etc.). *She's _____ artist.*
> Use _____ before consonant sounds (b, h, w, etc.). *He's _____ lawyer.*

see Reference page 13

3 Write *a* or *an*.

_a_ mother

1 ___ answer   2 ___ uncle   3 ___ hamburger   4 ___ taxi
5 ___ aunt   6 ___ number   7 ___ family   8 ___ handbag

Person to person

4 **a** Guess other students' jobs. Use a dictionary.

A: *Are you a taxi driver?*
B: *No, I'm not a taxi driver.*

A: *Are you a ...*
B: *Yes, I am./No, I'm not a ...*

b Ask and answer about your partner's family or friends.

> ~~brother~~   mother   father
> sister   uncle   best friend

A: Is your brother a manager?
B: No, he isn't. He's an accountant.

Grammar | *to be* (negative)

5 Complete the Active grammar box with *'m not* and *isn't*.

> ### Active grammar
>
> | | | |
> |---|---|---|
> | I | _____ | We aren't |
> | He | _____ | You aren't |
> | She | _____ | They aren't |

see Reference page 13

6 Complete the sentences with the correct negative form of *to be*.

We <u>aren't</u> from the United States.

1 My sister _____ married.
2 I _____ a shop assistant, I'm the manager!
3 My cousins are sixteen but they _____ at school.
4 Uncle John is old now but he _____ retired.
5 You _____ English. Where are you from?
6 I _____ unemployed; I'm retired.

Reading

7 Look at the form on the website. Match the questions to the parts of the form.

a How old are you? ☐3
b What's your (mobile) phone number? ☐
c What's your surname? ☐
d What's your email address? ☐
e Where are you from? ☐
f What's your job? ☐
g What's your first name? ☐
h What's your address? ☐
i What's your nationality? ☐

1. First name: Marta
2. Surname:
3. Age:
4. Place of origin:
5. Nationality:
6. Address:
7. Email address:
8. Telephone number
   (home):
   (mobile):
9. Occupation:

Listening

8 a ▮1.9▮ Listen. Who are Marta and Jake?

b Listen again and complete the form on the website.

c Check your answers with a partner.

A: *What's her surname?*
B: *Nowak. How old is she?*
A: *She's twenty-two.*

Speaking

9 Copy the form in Ex. 7. Ask your partner the questions to complete the form.

10 Work in pairs. Complete the forms.

Student A: ask and answer about the forms below.
Student B: look at page 125.

A: *OK. Let's start with Form A. Anne – what's her surname?*
B: *Simons – S-I-M-O-N-S.*
A: *What's her nationality?*

A

First name: `ANNE`
Surname:
Age: `3 4`
Place of origin: `VANCOUVER  CANADA`
Nationality:
Address: `12  HYTHE  STREET`
`LONDON`
Email address:

Telephone number (home): `0208142910055`
Telephone number (mobile):
Occupation: `LAWYER`

B

First name:
Surname: `MARSHALL`
Age:
Place of origin:
Nationality: `AUSTRALIAN`
Address:

Email address: `d.marshall@total.`
`com`
Telephone number (home):
Telephone number (mobile): `0795400068893`
Occupation:

1 Communication

Making conversation

1 **a** [1.10] Listen to two dialogues and tick (✓) the expressions you hear.

Excuse me ... ☐ See you later. ☐
Bye. ☐ Hello. ☐ Hi. ☐
Good morning. ☐
See you tomorrow. ☐ Goodbye. ☐

b Listen again. Complete the How to box.

start and finish a basic conversation

Start	Hello.
	_____
	_____
	_____
Finish	See you tomorrow.
	_____
	_____
	_____

2 **a** Complete the dialogues with the expressions in the box.

What's your job?
No, I'm not. I'm single.
I'm from Barcelona.
Hello Maria, I'm Clara.
Excuse me, are you Silvio?
What's your email address?

1 A: Hello, I'm Maria.
   B: _____
   A: Pleased to meet you.

2 A: _____
   B: Yes, I am. What's your name?
   A: My name's Jordi.

3 A: Where are you from?
   B: _____

4 A: _____
   B: It's silvio77@hotserve.com.

5 A: _____
   B: I'm a student at the university.

6 A: Are you married?
   B: _____

b [1.11] Listen and check your answers.

3 Practise the dialogues in Ex. 2a with a partner. Use real information!

4 **a** Match a–d to numbers on the application form.

a your birthday ___
b married or single ___
c exams and certificates ___
d name of a relative (husband or wife, mother or father) ___

Ⓢ Saver Bank plc

JOB APPLICATION FORM
Please complete in pen and sign at the bottom.

1 Surname: _____
2 First name: _____
3 Date of birth: _____ 4 Age: _____
5 Marital status: _____
6 Place of origin: _____
7 Nationality: _____
8 Passport or identity card number: _____
9 Address: _____
   _____
10 Email address: _____
11 Telephone number: _____
12 Occupation: _____
13 Qualifications: _____
14 Languages: _____
15 Next of kin: _____

Please sign here:

b Complete the form with information about *you*.

5 **a** Exchange your forms with other students. Find:

• a married student.
• a student with two languages.
• a student with the letter 'Y' in his/her name.
• a student with a university degree.
• a student with a different place of origin.

b Tell the class your results.

A: *Maria. She's married.*

Subject pronouns, possessive adjectives and possessive 's

There are eight subject pronouns in English. Use subject pronouns before verbs. There are also eight possessive adjectives. Use possessive adjectives before nouns.

Subject pronouns	*I* *you* *he* *she* *it* *we* *you* *they*	*+ verb*	Possessive adjectives	*my* *your* *his* *her* *its* *our* *your* *their*	*+ noun*

Possessive adjectives and noun + *'s* have the meaning *belongs to* (for things). With people they show relationships.

This is John's phone.   *This is **his** phone.*

Peggy is Al's wife.   *Peggy is **his** wife.*

Verb *to be*

⊕	*I*	*'m*	*German. / from Germany.*
	You	*'re*	
	He / She / It	*'s*	
	We / You / They	*'re*	
⊖	*I*	*'m not*	*Italian. / from Italy.*
	You	*aren't*	
	He / She / It	*isn't*	
	We / You / They	*aren't*	

❓	*Am*	*I*	*American?*	*Yes,* *(No,)*	*I*	*am.* *('m not)*
	Are	*you*			*you*	*are.* *(aren't)*
	Is	*he / she / it*			*he / she / it*	*is. (isn't)*
	Are	*we / you / they*			*we / you / they*	*are.* *(aren't)*

In informal English we usually use the contracted forms:
'm = am, 's = is, 're = are, isn't = is not, aren't = are not

*I am British. = **I'm** British. He is Brazilian. = **He's** Brazilian.*

*I'm not Italian. He/She/It **isn't** Italian. We/You/They **aren't** Italian.*

We don't use contracted forms in questions and short affirmative answers.

A: *Are you Russian?*   **B:** *Yes, I am.*

Wh- questions

We form *wh-* questions with a question word.

Who asks about a person.

What asks about a thing.

Where asks about a place.

How old asks about age.

Question word + *am/is/are* + subject pronoun.

***Where** are you from?*

***How old** is she?*

a/an

Use *a/an* to introduce singular nouns: *a teacher, an address.*

Use *a* before consonant sounds: *a burger, a handbag.*

Use *an* before vowel sounds: *an engineer, an uncle.*

Use *a/an* with nouns: *a doctor,* but we don't use *a/an* with adjectives: *she's unemployed*

Key vocabulary

Jobs

a bank clerk   an architect
a computer programmer
an artist   a dentist
an electrician   a doctor
an engineer   a housewife
an accountant   a househusband
a journalist   a judge   a lawyer
a nurse   a police officer
a secretary   a shop assistant
a student   a teacher
a traffic warden   a manager
a taxi driver   retired   unemployed

Family

Male:	Female:
father	mother
husband	wife
son	daughter
brother	sister
uncle	aunt
nephew	niece
grandfather	grandmother
stepfather	stepmother
father-in-law	mother-in-law

Male or female:

parents   children   cousins

1 Choose the correct word in italics.

Excuse me. Is this *my/your* bag?

1 John is twelve and *his/her* sister is fourteen.

2 This is Mariana. She's *my/her* wife's best friend.

3 Mr and Mrs Silva are teachers and *they/their* children are students.

4 We are German. *Our/Their* parents are from Frankfurt.

5 Jennifer López is American but *her/their* parents are from Puerto Rico.

6 My sister is married. *His/Her* husband is forty-three.

7 I am from Rio de Janeiro but *my/our* boyfriend is from El Salvador.

8 Tessa is married. *Her's/Tessa's* husband is Canadian.

9 Martin Sheen is a film star. Emilio Estevez and Charlie Sheen are *his/their* sons.

2 Make sentences.

Pilar and Esteban/Spain

Pilar and Esteban are from Spain.
They are Spanish.

1 Elizabeth/the United States

2 Ivan and Katia/Russia

3 I/France

4 You/Britain

5 Pavlos/Greece

6 His camera/Japan

7 I/Poland

3 Complete the questions and answers. Use information from Ex. 2.

A: (1) ___Is___ Elizabeth British?

B: No, she (2) _isn't_ . She's (3) _American_ .

A: (4) _____ Katia and Ivan from Mexico?

B: No, they (5) _____. They (6) _____ from (7) _____.

A: (8) _____ Pavlos (9) _____ Greece?

B: Yes, he (10) _____.

A: (11) _____ his camera German?

B: (12) _____, it (13) _____. It's Japanese.

4 Write about you. Correct the false sentences.

I'm an English student.

That's right.

I'm from the United States.

No, I'm not from the United States. I'm from ...

1 I'm seventeen years old.

2 My parents are doctors.

3 My best friend is a student.

4 Our teacher is British.

5 My mobile phone is German.

6 My brother/sister is married.

5 Complete the dialogue with questions.

A: *Hi, what's your name?*

B: My name's Andreas Schmidt.

A: (1) _____

B: Yes, it is, and Schmidt is my surname.

A: (2) _____

B: I'm from Germany.

A: (3) _____

B: I'm twenty-three.

A: (4) _____

B: I'm an engineer ... This is David and Gina.

A: (5) _____

B: They're my cousins.

A: (6) _____

B: No, they aren't. They're British. My aunt is married to a British man.

6 Write *a/an*.

_an_ American president

1 ___ email address

2 ___ Australian actor

3 ___ first name

4 ___ Polish surname

5 ___ Japanese television

6 ___ British taxi

7 ___ Italian car

7 Find the jobs and family words in the word chains, and write them in the table.

journalisteacheretiredentistaxidriver

cousinstudentrafficwardenursengineer

parentsoniecelectricianephew

JOBS	FAMILY
journalist	cousins
	parents

2 Activities

Lead-in

1 a Which activities can you see in the photos?

> go to work   leave work   have dinner   have lunch   get up
> go to bed   have breakfast   get home   leave home

b Match the activities from Ex. 1a to the parts of the day.

in the morning ___*get up,*___   in the evening _____

in the afternoon _____   at night _____

2 a **2.1** Listen and complete the times with these words.

> quarter past   half past   quarter to   o'clock

What time is it?

1 It's _____ six.   3 It's three _____.

2 It's _____ five.   4 It's _____ eight.

b What time is it? Complete the times then ask and answer.

1 It's _____ o'clock.   3 It's quarter to _____.

2 It's half past _____.   4 It's quarter past _____.

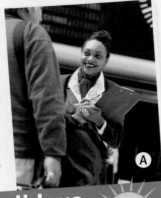

1

A fun job
for fun people!

Are you 18-25?
Be a rep for
Fun Club Holidays

- organise parties
- sell tickets for excursions
- help our clients

Call 0800 007007 now!

A

2

Fun Club Holidays
Fun package holidays
for young people age 18–30

B **C** **D** **E** **F**

Hotels, food and entertainment
included in the price!

Meet people, play games and have FUN

with FUN CLUB

Reading

1   Match the advertisements to the descriptions.

advertisement for a package holiday = ___

advertisement for a job = ___

Vocabulary | holidays

2   **a** Match the words to the pictures A–F.

1 restaurant ☐   2 swimming pool/games ☐
3 entertainment ☐   4 beach ☐
5 holiday rep and client ☐   6 nightclub ☐

b Read the advertisements and match the verbs to the nouns.

VERB	NOUN	ADVERTISEMENT
1 have	a games	____
2 organise	b people	____
3 sell	c fun	_2_
4 meet	d clients	____
5 play	e parties	____
6 help	f tickets	____

c Now match each word pair to an advertisement.

Listening

3   **a** **2.2** Jenny is a holiday rep. Listen and tick (✓) the eight activities she mentions.

1 Get up ☐
2 Have breakfast ☐
3 Go to the hotels ☐
4 Tell clients about parties ☐
5 Have lunch ☐
6 Go to the office ☐
7 Organise games at the pool ☐
8 Take clients to a restaurant ☐
9 Go to a nightclub ☐
10 Get home ☐

b Listen again. Write Jenny's activities and the times in the correct place in her diary.

Morning

1 *get up - 10.00.*

2 _____

3 _____

Afternoon

4 _____

5 _____

Evening

6 _____

7 _____

8 _____

Grammar | Present Simple: *I/you/we*

4 Look at the tapescript on page 150 and complete the Active grammar box.

Active grammar

⊕	*I meet the clients.*
	Sometimes we _____ special parties.
Yes/no questions	*Do you eat with the clients?*
	_____ the games?
	Yes, I _____.
	No, I _____.
Wh- questions	*What do you do in the afternoon?*
	Where _____ for dinner?

see Reference page 23

5 Match the questions and answers.

1 Where do you work?   a I watch TV.
2 What do you do?   b No, I don't.
3 When do you have   c I work in a school.
   lunch?   d At half past one.
4 Do you have lunch   e I'm a teacher.
   in a restaurant?
5 What do you do in
   the evening?

6 a Read the interview. Complete the dialogue and write the job at the end.

A: When (1) _____ you get up?
B: At ten in the evening.
A: (2) _____ you work at night?
B: Yes, I do.
A: What (3) _____ you (4) _____ in the afternoon?
B: I sleep.
A: (5) _____ do you have dinner?
B: I (6) _____ dinner at about eleven in the morning.
A: Do (7) _____ work in an office?
B: No, I (8) _____.
A: Where (9) _____ you work?
B: I (10) _____ in a hospital.
A: So, what do you do?
B: I'm a ⬚⬚⬚⬚⬚⬚.

b **2.3** Listen and check your answers. Then practise the dialogue with a partner.

7 Look at Jenny's diary in Ex. 3b. Make a diary about your daily routines.

8 Complete the How to box. Use the information from Ex. 6.

HOW TO... | **talk about your daily routine**

Ask about routines	*What _____ you _____ in the afternoon?*
Answer	*I sleep.*
Ask about times	*When _____ you get up?*
Answer	*_____ ten in the evening.*
Ask about places	*Where _____ you work?*
Answer	*I _____ in a hospital.*

Person to person

9 Interview a partner.

• What do you do in the morning?
• When do you go to work/school?
• Do you work in an office?

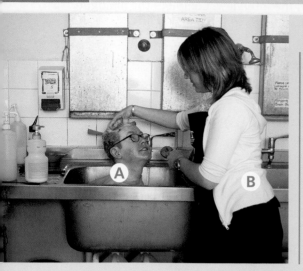

Jo Kinsey has an interesting job. She's a *hairdresser* – but a very special hairdresser. Jo works at Madame Tussaud's – the *wax model* museum. She starts work at 7.30. In the morning she checks the models for dirty hair and in the afternoon she washes and dries their hair.

Jeanette Ewart is a cleaner, but in a very dangerous place. She cleans the *shark tank* in the zoo in her city. She swims under the water every day to clean the tank, and she feeds the *sharks* three times a week. She's careful, but another diver waits by the tank and watches her. The visitors at the zoo watch her too.

John Wardley is an inventor. He invents exciting rides for his theme park. He walks through the theme park and he listens to people when they talk about a *ride*. He invents new rides, and the engineers make the rides. John likes his work – his theme park is the best place to work!

Reading

1   **a** Look at the photos. What are the jobs?

b Read the texts quickly and check your answers.

c Match A–E on the photos to the words in the texts in italics.

A _____   B _____
C _____   D _____
E _____

2   Write Jo, John or Jeanette.

This person ...
works under water. *Jeanette*

1   works in a museum.
2   thinks a lot at work.
3   starts work before eight o'clock.
4   listens to other people.
5   is very careful at work.

Vocabulary | verbs

3   Write a verb from the texts under each picture.

a

b

c

d

e

f

g

Grammar | Present Simple: *he/she/it*

4 **a** Complete the sentences with the correct form of the verbs in brackets.

1 Jo _____ (wash) and _____ (dry) the models' hair.

2 Jeanette _____ (clean) the shark tank.

3 Jo _____ (have) an interesting job.

b Complete the Active grammar box with *has, -s, -es* or *-ies*.

Active grammar

After *he, she* and *it,* add _____, but:

1 when the verb ends in *o, s, sh, ch* or *x,* add _____.

2 when the verb ends in consonant + *y,* omit *-y* and add _____.

3 the form of *have* after *he, she* and *it* is _____.

---

see Reference page 23

c Look at the texts. Which form of the verb do we use after *they* (e.g. the engineers)?

5 Complete the sentences with the correct form of the verbs in the box.

> clean   have   help   play   talk   wash   watch

1 My mother _____ our house.

2 The teacher _____ in English in class.

3 Jake _____ his hair every morning.

4 Matt _____ DVDs on his laptop computer.

5 Allie _____ her little sister with her homework.

6 My brothers _____ football every evening.

7 They _____ dangerous jobs.

Pronunciation

6 **a** **2.4** Listen to the endings of these three verbs. Are they all the same?

/s/ walks	/z/ listens	/ɪz/ organises

b **2.5** Listen and write the verbs in the table. Then repeat them.

Listening

7 **a** Complete the dialogue.

A: Does Jeanette like her work?

B: Yes, she does. She *loves* it.

A: _____ she clean the tank every day?

B: Yes, she _____.

A: _____ she feed the sharks every day?

B: No. She _____ them three times a week.

A: _____ she work every day?

B: No. She _____ five days a week.

b **2.6** Listen and check your answers.

8 Cross out the incorrect words in the questions.

1 *Does/Do* the sharks *eat/eats* every day?

2 *Does/Do* Jeanette *clean/cleans* the tank every day?

3 *Does/Do* Jeanette *like/likes* her work?

9 Complete the questions with the verbs in brackets.

Do you *work* every day? (work)

1 _____ Maria _____ her work? (like)

2 _____ your parents _____ DVDs? (watch)

3 _____ John _____ computer games? (invent)

4 _____ I _____ in my sleep? (talk)

5 _____ Anna _____ children? (have)

Speaking

10 Rob is a studio engineer. Ask and answer about his daily routine.

Student A: look at the diary on page 125.

Student B: look at the diary on page 129.

Writing

11 Write about part of Rob's day.

1 Choose morning, afternoon or evening.

2 Underline the verbs in the diary for that part of the day.

3 Write sentences with the verbs. Use *and* or *or* to join sentences.

Rob gets up at eight o' clock and he has breakfast.

Vocabulary | everyday objects and colours

1 **a** Look at the photo. Where are the people? What do they do here?

   b **2.7** Listen and check your answers.

2 **a** Label the things in the picture.

> bags books watches DVD player
> laptop computer pictures shoes lamps
> suitcase video camera

fax machine   printer   ⑧

① ⑤

dishes

chair

③ ⑥ ⑩
④ ⑦ ⑨

   b **2.8** Listen and tick (✓) the things you hear.

3 Find examples of the colours in the pictures.

> ~~black~~ yellow grey brown white pink red
> orange blue purple green silver gold

The fax machine is black.

Grammar | *this, that, these, those*

4 **a** **2.9** Listen and complete the dialogues.

1

A: What's _____?   **B:** It's _____.

2

A: What's _____?   **B:** It's _____.

3
A: What are _____?   **B:** They're _____.

4

A: What are _____?   **B:** They're _____.

see Reference page 23

   b Correct the underlined words in the sentences.

What <u>are</u> this? *What's this?*
<u>These are</u> a car. *This is a car.*

1   What colour is <u>those</u>?
2   These <u>is</u> very beautiful.
3   <u>Are</u> that your house?
4   <u>These</u> isn't very old.

Pronunciation

5 **a** **2.10** Listen to the vowel sounds. Repeat.

/ɪ/ this   /iː/ these

b **2.11** Listen and write these words in the table.

> green   listen   niece   pink   read
> sister   teacher   think

/ɪ/ this	/iː/ these

Vocabulary | adjectives

6 **a** Check these adjectives in a dictionary. Match the opposites.

> ~~bad~~ big ~~good~~ horrible modern nice old old-fashioned small useful useless young

bad – good

b Write sentences about you with six of the adjectives.

My house is big but my car is small.

Listening

7 **a** **2.12** Listen. Where are the people?

b Listen again. Match the dialogues to the pictures below.

c Look at the tapescript on page 151. Find six more words for everyday objects.

A

B

C

Grammar | noun plurals

8 **a** Complete the Active grammar box.

> ### Active grammar
>
> *one book, twenty* _____
>
> *one lamp, ten* _____
>
> *one phone, two* _____
>
> To make the regular plural of a noun, add _____.

see Reference page 23

b Some nouns change their spelling in the plural, and others are irregular. Write the plurals of these words.

regular	book → *books*, bag → _____, camera → _____, shoe → _____
word + -es	watch → _____, dish → _____
f → -ves	scarf → _____
consonant – -y → -ies	diary → *diaries*
irregular	person → *people*

Lifelong learning

Irregular plurals

Use a dictionary to find irregular plurals:

> **diary** /ˈdaɪəri/ noun, plural **diaries**

c Find the plurals of these words and write them in the table in Ex. 8b.

> man woman child wife dictionary address family niece class bus

Speaking

9 Play a guessing game.

Student A: think of an object, e.g. my mobile phone.

Student B: ask *yes/no* questions. Guess the object. Use adjectives.

B: *Is it old-fashioned?*

Holiday routines

1 Match the photos to the captions.

1 In the city ☐
2 In the mountains ☐
3 At the beach ☐

2 a Complete the questions in the questionnaire with words from the box.

> do do get ~~go~~ go time what when ~~where~~ who

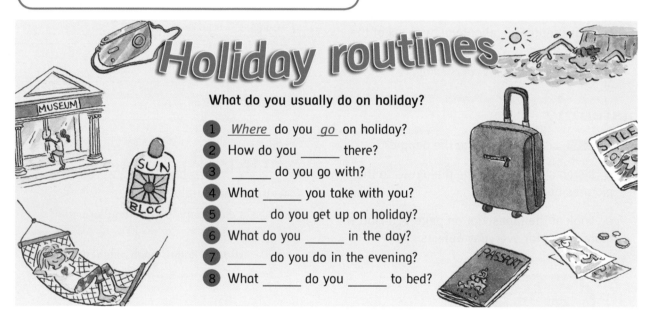

Holiday routines

What do you usually do on holiday?

1 _Where_ do you _go_ on holiday?
2 How do you _____ there?
3 _____ do you go with?
4 What _____ you take with you?
5 _____ do you get up on holiday?
6 What do you _____ in the day?
7 _____ do you do in the evening?
8 What _____ do you _____ to bed?

b Match the questions to these answers.

a my camera and a good book _4_
b to the beach ___
c at about ten in the morning ___
d go on excursions or swim ___
e at about half past eleven ___
f go to a nightclub or restaurant ___
g my friends ___
h by car ___

c What do you do? Answer the questions in the questionnaire in Ex. 2a.

3 a Ask your partner about his/her holiday routines and write the answers.

A: *Where do you go on holiday?*
B: *I go to my sister's house.*

b Choose the best holiday from the photos for your partner.

4 a Tell the class about your partner's holiday routines.

Stefano goes to his sister's house in the city. He takes the bus. He goes with his wife ...

b Make sentences about your partner's holiday routines.

Present Simple

⊕	I we you they	take
	he she it	takes

*I **take** the train.*

*She **takes** the bus.*

Use the Present Simple for daily routines and activities. With *I, we, you* and *they* the Present Simple form is the same as the infinitive. With *he, she* and *it* we add *-s* to the infinitive, but note these exceptions.

- verbs ending in *-ch, -s, -sh, -x* and *-o* add *-es*:

  watch → watches, go → goes

- verbs ending in *-y*, remove *-y* and add *-ies*:

  carry → carries

- *have → has*

Wh- questions

- Wh- word + *do* + *I/we/you/they* + infinitive

  When do you finish work?

- Wh- word + *does* + *he/she/it* + infinitive

  Where does he eat lunch?

- In questions, don't add *-s* to the verb.

Yes/no questions

- *Do* + *I/we/you/they* + infinitive

  Do you eat with the clients?

- *Does* + *he/she/it* + infinitive

  Does he finish at five o' clock?

- Note the short answers:

  Yes, I/we/you/they do.
  he/she/it does.

  No, I/we/you/they don't.
  he/she/it doesn't.

this, that, these, those

	Singular	Plural
Near	this	these
Far	that	those

What's **this**?   Do you like **these** shoes?   Look at **that** car!   **Those** bags are horrible.

Noun plurals

We add *-s* to nouns to make the regular noun plural:

book → books, picture → pictures

There are some special rules.

- nouns ending *-ch, -s, -sh, -x* add *-es*:

  watch → watches, address → addresses

- most nouns ending *-f*, remove *-f* and add *-ves*:

  scarf → scarves, knife → knives

- nouns ending consonant + *-y*, remove *-y* and add *-ies*:

  diary → diaries, city → cities

Note: nouns ending with a vowel + *-y* are regular: *day → days*

Some plural nouns are completely irregular:

man → men, child → children

Key vocabulary

Personal possessions

bag book camera car chair desk diary dish DVD player handbag fax machine lamp laptop computer magazine mobile phone picture printer scarf scissors shoes suitcase wallet watch

Basic verbs/verb phrases

Routines:

eat work watch sleep get up go to work/school/bed have breakfast/lunch/dinner leave home/work start finish wash clean

Other verbs:

check dry feed help invent like make meet open organise play repair sell swim wait walk

1 Look at the pictures and write sentences about Clive's day. Use the verbs and phrases in the boxes.

> watch   finish   eat   go   read   ~~get~~

> a sandwich   the news   work   to bed
> ~~the bus to work~~   his emails

A   *He gets the bus to work at quarter past eight.*

2 Complete the sentences and questions with the correct form of the verbs in brackets.

She *finishes* work at five o'clock. (finish)

1   They _____ at ten o'clock on Sundays. (get up)
2   _____ he _____ a good job? (have)
3   I _____ to English lessons in the evening. (go)
4   She _____ the house in the morning. (clean)
5   What _____ you _____ on Saturday afternoons? (do)

3 Put the words in the correct order to make questions.

to you work When go do

When do you go to work?

1   she afternoon What does do in the ?
2   have Where does lunch he ?
3   to work Do take the train you ?
4   does finish he When work ?
5   What in you evening do do the ?

4 Six of these plural nouns are wrong. Find five more and correct them.

lunchs	✗ *lunches*	4 pizzaes	_____
clients	✔ _____	5 sandwichs	_____
1 holidaies	_____	6 sharks	_____
2 hotels	_____	7 studios	_____
3 partys	_____	8 knifes	_____

5 Complete the questions. Then write the answers.

What's _this_ ?
It's a _laptop computer_ .

What are _____?
They're _____.

What's _____?
It's a _____.

_____?
_____.

_____?
_____.

6 **a** Look at the 'personal possessions' vocabulary on page 23. Copy the table and write the objects.

PERSONAL	HOUSE/HOME	TRAVEL	EQUIPMENT
diary	chair	car	DVD player

b Look at the 'routines' vocabulary on page 23. Write the verbs in the order you do them during the day.

1   *get up*   2   *wash*   3   *have breakfast*

c Who does these things in their work? Write the jobs.

organises people on holiday _holiday rep_

1   washes people's hair _____
2   repairs cars _____
3   sells things in a shop _____
4   invents and makes machines _____
5   helps students at school _____
6   cleans the house _____
7   works in a bank _____

A

B

C

D

3 Free time

Lead-in

1 **a** Match the photos to verbs and verb phrases in the box.

cook   dance   go for a walk   go shopping   go to a concert
go to the gym   listen to music   meet friends   play football
play the guitar   read a book or magazine   sunbathe   swim
watch TV or a video

b Check the meanings of the verbs in the box with a partner.

A: *What does 'cook' mean?*

B: *It means make food, for example, lunch or dinner.*

c Where do you do the activities in Ex. 1a? Write them in the table.

AT HOME	IN THE PARK	AT THE SHOPS	AT A NIGHTCLUB	AT A CONCERT HALL	AT A SPORTS CENTRE/SWIMMING POOL

2 **a** Write two activities that you do, where you do them and when.

b Ask your partner questions.

What activity do you do? Where do you do it? When do you do it?

c Tell the class about your partner.

Mark plays the piano. He plays at home...

TRAFFIC JAMS. WE HATE THEM, BUT WHAT DO WE DO IN THEM?

Listening

1 Look at the photo and answer the questions.

1 When does this happen in your town/city?

2 What do you do in traffic jams?

2 **a** ▶ 3.1 Complete the quotes below. Compare your answers with a partner, then listen and check.

> 'Traffic jams are OK. I think about work and _plan_ my day. I (1)_____ my diary. <u>My daughter doesn't like traffic jams</u> – she calls her friends, but I don't make phone calls in the car. It's dangerous.' (*Melanie, 39*)
>
> • • • • • • • • •
>
> 'Well, in the mornings I shave and listen to the radio. I (2)_____ the news. I like music, but unfortunately my car doesn't have a CD player.' (*Nathan, 28*)
>
> • • • • • • • • •
>
> 'I don't do a lot, really. I (3)_____ traffic jams – they're so boring! I think about things or (4)_____ the people in the other cars. Sometimes I sing.' (*Simon, 35*)
>
> • • • • • • • • •
>
> 'We (5)_____ computer games or (6)_____ friends on our mobiles. Or we just talk. We don't like the radio.' (*Lauren, 22 and Emily, 21*)

b Mark the sentences true (T) or false (F).

Melanie makes phone calls in a traffic jam. *F*

1 Melanie's daughter likes traffic jams.

2 Nathan listens to CDs.

3 Simon sings in his car.

4 Lauren and Emily work on their computers.

5 Lauren and Emily think mobile phones in cars are dangerous.

Grammar | Present Simple: negative

3 **a** Find the negative of the sentences below in the texts. <u>Underline</u> them.

1 My daughter likes traffic jams.

2 I make phone calls in the car.

3 My car has a CD player.

4 We like the radio.

b Complete the Active grammar box with *don't* or *doesn't*.

Active grammar

I	_____	
He/She/It	_____	work.
We/You/They	_____	

---

see Reference page 33

4 **a** Correct the false sentences in Ex. 2b. Use the negative verb form.

Melanie doesn't make phone calls in a traffic jam.

b What about you? Tick (✓) the true sentences. Correct the false sentences.

I like traffic jams.   *I don't like traffic jams.*

1 I listen to the news on the radio.

2 I write my diary every day.

3 I play football at the weekend.

4 I make phone calls in the car.

5 I sleep for ten hours every night.

Vocabulary | days of the week

5 **a** ▪3.2▪ Number the days of the week in the correct order. Then listen and check.

☐ Friday ☐ Monday ☐ Saturday 1 Sunday
☐ Thursday ☐ Tuesday ☐ Wednesday

b ▪3.3▪ Listen to Alistair talking about his lunchtime activities. Write the days.

C

Tuesday

A

D

B

E

F

Reading

6 **a** Read the text about Alistair. Find three mistakes with the days and correct them.

What I do
in my lunch **break**

Today we talk to Alistair Standing. Alistair works in the city. He doesn't go home at lunchtime, so how does he spend his time?

'Well, I have an hour and I want to use that time. I do a lot of different things,' says Alistair. He certainly does! On Mondays Alistair goes for a walk or he has a swim. On Tuesdays he sometimes meets friends and they have lunch in a restaurant. On Wednesdays he goes to the gym. On Thursdays he sometimes listens to a lunchtime concert. On Fridays he goes shopping. On Sundays he watches football on TV and sleeps!

b Write positive or negative sentences about Alistair. Use the corrected text to help you.

Mondays/play tennis

He doesn't play tennis on Mondays.

1 Thursdays/watch a film
2 Fridays/work
3 Saturdays/play football
4 Sundays/sleep

Speaking

7 **a** Read the questionnaire. Tick (✓) the things you do, and write the day you do them, if possible. Then add two more.

Activity	You (when)	Your partner (when)
talk to friends on the phone		
watch TV		
listen to music		
play computer games		
go for walks		
play a sport		
go to concerts	✓ (Friday evenings)	
go to the cinema		
read books		
go to the gym		
_____		
_____		

b Complete the questionnaire for your partner.

A: *Do you go to concerts?*

B: *Yes, I sometimes go to concerts on Friday evenings./No, I don't.*

Writing

8 **a** What do you do in your free time? Make a list.

Monday evenings – watch TV
Saturdays – read newspaper/go shopping

b Write a short article about your free time. Use your notes from Ex. 8a.

1 Start your article with a short introduction.

My name is ... I work in ..., but I do a lot of things in my free time. On Mondays I ...

2 Write your notes into sentences.

On Monday evenings I (sometimes) watch TV.

3 Join some of the sentences with *and, or* or *but*.

On Saturday mornings I read the newspaper or I go shopping.

4 Combine your introduction and sentences to write your article.

3.2 Skateboard style

Grammar	*can/can't*
Can do	talk about what you can and can't do

Vocabulary | sports and games

1 **a** Match the words from the box to the activities.

> aerobics computer games football running
> judo sailing skiing swimming tennis yoga

b Write the activities in the table. Then check in the Reference on page 33.

DO	GO	PLAY
do aerobics	*go running*	*play football*

c Ask and answer.

A: *Do you do yoga?*
B: *Yes, I do.*
A: *When?*
B: *On Thursday evenings.*

Tony Hawk
the man and the champion

Tony Hawk is American. He's 34. He's married. He has three children. He's a businessman. And he's the skateboarding champion of the world.

Reading

2 **a** Look at the photo. Answer the questions.

1 Do you go skateboarding?
2 What kind of people usually go skateboarding? (young/old)

b Read the introduction to the text above and answer the questions.

1 Where is Tony Hawk from?
2 What does he do?
3 Some people think he is unusual. Why?

3 **a** Look at the text (page 29) and find these things.

1 Tony's age   2 his son's name and age
3 the name of Tony's book

b Read the introduction and the text again and answer the questions. Write sentences.

How many children does Tony have?
He has three children.

1 How many prizes does he have?
2 What does he do on his skateboard?
3 What does his son ride?
4 Where does Tony take his show?
5 What do the people in the show do?

Tony has 73 prizes from skateboarding competitions. He's 34 but he can skateboard like a sixteen year old. He goes very fast and he does tricks on his skateboard. His four-year-old son, Spencer, can also ride a skateboard!

But Tony isn't only a fantastic skateboarder – he can do other things too. Tony writes computer games and books. Lots of people buy his books. *HAWK – Occupation: skateboarder* is a bestseller in the United States.

Tony also has a skateboarding and music show and he takes it all around the United States and Canada. Tony doesn't perform the music – he can't play the guitar or sing – but he and other skateboarders perform tricks, and their musicians play rock music. The show is very popular.

Grammar | can/can't

4 a Tick (✓) the things Tony can do. Cross (✗) the things he can't do.

play the guitar	☐	ride a skateboard	☐
use a computer	☐	sing	☐
play rock music	☐	perform tricks	☐

b Complete the sentences and questions with *can* or *can't*. Then complete the Active grammar box.

What _can_ Tony Hawk do?

1 He _____ ride a skateboard.

2 What _____ his friends do?

3 They _____ play the guitar and sing.

4 _____ you ride a skateboard?

5 No, I _____, but I _____ ride a bicycle.

Active grammar

➕ I/You/He/She/It/We/They _____ swim.

➖ I/You/He/She/It/We/They _____ swim.

❓ _____ I/you/he/she/it/we/they swim?

Yes, I/you/he/she/it/we/they <u>can</u>.

No, I/you/he/she/it/we/they _____.

see Reference page 33

Pronunciation

5 **3.4** Listen. What can Jonny and Susie do? Tick (✓) the things they can do.

	Jonny	Susie
play the guitar	✓	✓
play the piano		
sing		
dance		
play football		
play tennis		
ski		
speak French		
speak Spanish		
ride a bike		
drive a car		

6 a **3.5** We say *can/can't* in different ways. Listen and repeat.

/ə/	/æ/	/ɑː/
<u>Can</u> you dance?	Yes, I <u>can</u>.	No, I <u>can't</u>.

b Ask and answer. Use the table.

A: *Can Susie speak French?*

B: *Yes, she can.*

A: *Can Jonny drive?*

B: *No, he can't.*

c Work with a partner. Ask and answer, using the activities in Ex. 5.

A: *Can you ski?*

B: *No, I can't. Can you ...?*

Speaking

7 a Work in groups. Find someone who ...

can ...
- speak three languages
- stand on their head
- write backwards
- move their ears
- play an unusual instrument
- write computer programs

can't ...
- cook
- swim
- write with their right hand
- get up in the mornings
- send a text message
- use a video or DVD player

b Tell the class about your group.

3.3 | Phone fun

Functions	making suggestions; using the phone
Can do	understand and leave a simple phone message

Listening

1 Do you use a mobile phone? Where? When? Who do you call?

2 **a** **3.6** Listen. Match the messages to the names.

Damian ☐   Jane 1   Mary Wilde ☐
Benson Cameras ☐   Steve Henshaw ☐

b Listen again and complete the messages with one word, a number or a time.

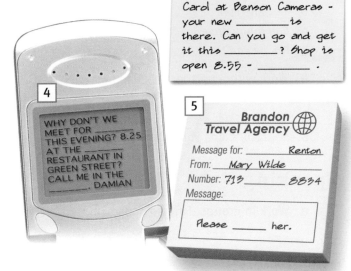

1
Message for: _Tony_
From: _____
Message:
Meet outside the _____ at 7.50.

2
Message for Mandy from Steve Henshaw.
Please _____ him - 068 919 _____.

3
Message for Michael _____.
Carol at Benson Cameras - your new _____ is there. Can you go and get it this _____? Shop is open 8.55 - _____.

4
WHY DON'T WE MEET FOR _____ THIS EVENING? 8.25 AT THE _____ RESTAURANT IN GREEN STREET? CALL ME IN THE _____. DAMIAN

5
Brandon Travel Agency
Message for: _____ Renton
From: _Mary Wilde_
Number: 713 _____ 8834
Message:
Please _____ her.

c Listen to message five again. How do we say *88* in the phone number?

3 **a** **3.7** Number the sentences in the correct order. Then listen and check.

OK. What's your number? ☐
OK. Bye. ☐
She isn't here right now. Can I take a message? ☐
Hello. 1
Yes, please ask her to phone Jeffrey. ☐
It's 011 908 5561. ☐
Hello, can I speak to Laura, please? ☐

b Practise the dialogue with a partner.

4 Make two phone calls.

Student A: turn to page 125.

Student B: read the notes below.

Call 1 Your name is Carla. Phone Student A: You want to speak to Jason. Your number is 990 675 3551.

Call 2 Answer the phone and start the conversation. (Sylvia isn't here today. Take a message for Sylvia.)

Reading

5 **a** Read the text below quickly. Match the headings to paragraphs 1–3.

a The Mobile Phone Olympics
b The phone throwing competition
c Texting in Britain

b Read the text again. Match the numbers to the information.

1	1.54 billion	a	words in Natalie's text message
2	50 million	b	Natalie's age
3	2 million	c	competitors
4	8	d	messages a month
5	15,000	e	messages an hour
6	18	f	messages a day for each user
7	30	g	messages a day

Texting at the Mobile Phone Olympics

1 In Britain people send 1.54 billion text messages every month. That's more than 50 million messages a day or 2 million an hour! In fact, the average mobile phone user sends about 8 messages a day.

2 Now texting fans have the chance to show what they can do at the Mobile Phone Olympics. Every year about 15,000 competitors enter the competition in London. In the texting event competitors send an 80-character message as fast as they can. This year's champion is 18-year-old Natalie Johnson from Leeds. She can send a 30-word text message in just 138 seconds!

3 Of course, some people hate mobile phones. One event at the Olympics is just for them. This is the 'Mobile Phone Throwing' competition. In this event competitors throw their phones as far as they can. It's a lot of fun for mobile phone haters!

6 `3.8` How do we say these numbers? Choose from the words in the box. Then listen and check your answers.

6 *six* 16 60 600 6,000 60,000 600,000 6,000,000 6,000,000,000

> six million   six thousand   sixty
> sixty thousand   six billion   ~~six~~
> six hundred thousand   six hundred   sixteen

Pronunciation

7 **a** `3.9` Listen. Underline the strong sounds.

sixteen   sixty
fourteen   forty

b `3.10` Listen and tick (✓) the number you hear.

1	fourteen	☐	forty	☐
2	eighteen	☐	eighty	☐
3	seventeen	☐	seventy	☐
4	thirteen	☐	thirty	☐
5	nineteen	☐	ninety	☐
6	sixteen	☐	sixty	☐

c Test your partner.

8 Look at page 152 and complete the How to box with examples from the dialogues in Ex. 2a.

HOW TO …

make suggestions and requests

Make suggestions	*Let's* + infinitive *Let's meet outside the cinema at ten to eight.*
	Why don't we + infinitive + ? _____
	How about + noun + ? _____
Make requests	*Can you* + infinitive + ? _____

see Reference page 33

9 **a** Find these times in the tapescript on page 152 and write them in words.

7.50   *ten to eight*

1	3.20 _____	2	8.55 _____
3	6.30 _____	4	8.25 _____

b Complete these suggestions and requests. Write the times in words.

we meet – cinema – 7.00?
Why *don't we meet at the cinema at seven*?

1   have dinner – Chinese restaurant – 8.40
    Let's _____

2   you come – the office tomorrow – 9.55?
    Can _____?

3   3.10 – Greek café – Belmont Street?
    How _____?

4   we go – the bar – 10.45?
    Why _____?

10 **a** What can people do in your town in the evening? Tick (✓) the activities and make notes about where and when you can do them.

see a film ☐   have dinner at a restaurant ☐
go to a football match ☐   go to a bar ☐
go to a nightclub ☐   go to a concert ☐
get a takeaway meal ☐
go to the sports centre ☐

b Work in pairs. You want to do something together tonight. Make suggestions.

A: *What can we do tonight?*

B: *Let's …*

A: *OK. Let's meet at half past nine./No, I don't like … How about …?*

3 Communication

The perfect job

1 a Match the abilities to the jobs. Use a dictionary.

ABILITIES	JOBS
1 speak foreign languages	a sports teacher
2 design buildings	b taxi driver
3 play sports	c artist
4 drive	d carpenter
5 repair computers	e mechanic
6 play a musical instrument	f photographer
7 draw and paint	g tourist guide
8 repair cars	h musician
9 use a camera	i architect
10 make things in wood	j computer technician

b Work with a partner. Think of more abilities and jobs.

2 a Read the information below about Jane and Brian. Complete their agency notes on the right.

> Jane Danby is thirty-two years old. She has a degree in Art from Edinburgh University. She can speak Spanish and German. She can paint and draw. She likes the Internet. She takes digital photos and she changes them on her computer. She can't drive.

> Brian Winter doesn't have any qualifications but he can do a lot of things. He can repair cars and engines, and he can repair houses. He doesn't like cold weather. He makes furniture in wood and metal. He is twenty-five years old and he has a driving licence.

b 3.11 Listen and complete the notes for David and Lizzie.

3 a Work in groups. You work for the Perfect Employment Agency. Jane, Brian, David and Lizzie want new jobs. Choose the best job for each person. Talk about your reasons and complete the table.

A: *I think 'computer technician' is best for Jane.*

B: *Do you? Why?*

A: *Because she likes the Internet ...*

NAME	JANE	BRIAN	DAVID	LIZZIE
JOB	computer technician			
REASONS	She likes the Internet.			

b Compare your ideas with other groups.

PERFECT EMPLOYMENT AGENCY

Applicant notes

NAME: .....Jane Danby.....

AGE: ....

QUALIFICATIONS: ....

ABILITIES: ....

LIKES/DISLIKES: ....

PERFECT EMPLOYMENT AGENCY

Applicant notes

NAME: .....Brian Winter.....

AGE: ....

QUALIFICATIONS: ....

ABILITIES: ....

LIKES/DISLIKES: ....

PERFECT EMPLOYMENT AGENCY

Applicant notes

NAME: .....David Burford.....

AGE: ....

QUALIFICATIONS: ....

ABILITIES: ....

LIKES/DISLIKES: ....

PERFECT EMPLOYMENT AGENCY

Applicant notes

NAME: .....Lizzie Pereira.....

AGE: ....

QUALIFICATIONS: ....

ABILITIES: ....

LIKES/DISLIKES: ....

Present Simple: negative

Form the negative of the Present Simple with the verb *do* + *not* + infinitive.

I You We They	don't (do not)	work.
He She It	doesn't (does not)	

*I **don't live** in the city.*
*She **doesn't work** in the office.*

Note that we do not add *-s* to the infinitive in the Present Simple negative.

can/can't

Can is a modal verb. We use modal verbs before other verbs.

The negative of *can* is *cannot,* but we usually use the short form *can't.*

I You He She It We You They	can can't (cannot)	sing.

Modal verbs do not change their form after *he*, *she* or *it*.

He can play the piano.

Use *can* and *can't* to talk about ability. Use *can* to talk about things we are able to do, and *can't* to talk about things that we are not able to do.

*I **can sing** but **I can't dance**.*

Use *can* + *you* + infinitive to make requests – when we want someone else to do something.

***Can you take** a message?*

Making suggestions

When we want to do something with another person we make suggestions.

Let's + infinitive
***Let's meet** outside the cinema at ten to eight.*
Why don't we + infinitive + ?
***Why don't we have** dinner this evening?*
How about + noun + ?
***How about lunch** on Friday?*

play, do, go + activities

Use *play* + noun for games, and for sports we usually do in teams, e.g. *play football, computer games*.

Use *do* + noun for activities we can do alone (not in a team), e.g. *do aerobics, yoga*.

Use *go* with activity verbs that end in *-ing*, e.g. *go swimming, running*.

Key vocabulary

Days of the week
Sunday   Monday   Tuesday   Wednesday   Thursday   Friday   Saturday

Activities
cook
dance
do aerobics/judo/yoga
drive a car
get a takeaway meal
go for a walk
go running/sailing/shopping/skiing/swimming
go to the cinema/a concert/the gym/a nightclub/
   a football match/a bar
have lunch/dinner (at a restaurant)
listen to music/the news/the radio
meet friends
play computer games/football/tennis
play the guitar/piano
read a book/a magazine/a newspaper
ride a bike
see a film
sing
skateboard
sunbathe
swim
watch a DVD/a video/the TV

1 Make positive or negative sentences about Malcolm.

live in a nice house

Malcolm doesn't live in a nice house.

sleep in the park

Malcolm sleeps in the park.

1 have a job
2 have an address
3 go to work every morning
4 carry his things in a bag
5 eat in restaurants
6 like his life

2 Write four sentences about the activities that you and your friends <u>don't</u> do together. Choose from the box.

> watch TV   go to a nightclub   go to the gym
> listen to music   eat in restaurants
> go to concerts   play a sport   go to the cinema
> play computer games   go shopping

We don't eat in restaurants.

1 _____   3 _____
2 _____   4 _____

3 Write a sentence with *can* and *can't* about the things below. Choose from the box.

> check spellings   drive   invent text messages
> play computer games   sleep all day
> play football   run   send photos   swim   think

Young children

can play computer games but they can't drive.

1 Computers
2 Sharks
3 Mobile phones
4 Cats

4 The text has eight mistakes. Find the mistakes and correct them.

> Andreas cans do a lot of things. He likes sports and he can plays basketball and football but he no can play tennis. He don't like tennis. He likes rock music and he play the guitar in shows. He sing too but he doesn't dances. He can't plays the piano.

5 Put the words in order to make suggestions and requests.

cinema to we tonight Why don't go the ?

Why don't we go to the cinema tonight?

1 six o'clock Let's at meet .
2 restaurant How the lunch at about Italian ?
3 a Can message you take ?
4 from takeaway Let's a McDonald's get .
5 give your Can number you me phone ?
6 we video don't watch this Why a evening ?
7 Saturday about on How dinner ?

6 Complete the diary with the correct verbs.

Monday

play football with the boys
1 _____ to the cinema (evening)

Tuesday

2 _____ Jack and Ellie for lunch
3 _____ the bikes to the park

Wednesday

4 _____ to the gym
5 _____ dinner for Emma

Thursday

6 _____ to a nightclub
7 _____ the piano for Sam

Friday

8 _____ yoga with Jane (morning)
9 _____ swimming with the girls

Saturday

10 _____ shopping

Sunday

11 _____ Harry's video

4 Food

Lead-in

1   Match eight words from the box to the things in the pictures.

> apples   beef   bread   butter   cheese   cherries   chicken
> eggs   milk   potatoes   rice   sugar   tea   trout   watermelon

2   **a** In pairs, find the meanings of the other words. Then complete the table below with all the food words you know.

MEAT/FISH	DAIRY	FRUIT	DRINKS	OTHER
			water	

b Where do you buy food? How do you pay for it?

3   Match the pictures below with the words from the box. Ask and answer the questions.

> coin   note   cheque   receipt   credit card

1   Which pictures show cash? When do you use cash/credit cards/cheques?
2   How much money do you have in your wallet? How much does this book cost? How much does your journey to school cost?

I've got three euros fifty in my wallet.

4.1 | Shopping lists

Grammar	countable and uncountable nouns; *How much?/How many?*
Can do	talk about quantities and numbers

Food around the world

Regan Ronayne and Craig Caven and their children, Andrea (5) and Ryan (3), live in California. They are a typical American family. Regan and Craig both work and they don't usually have time to cook, so they like convenience food. The children love hot dogs, cereal and cola. They eat at fast food restaurants once a week.

The Ukitas live in Tokyo, Japan. Kazuo Ukita lives with his wife, Sayo, and his daughters Mio (17) and Maya (14). He works in a bookshop. Sayo cooks breakfast before Kazuo leaves for work at 7.00 a.m. They have dinner together at home in the evenings. They eat a lot of fish and rice. Sayo cooks all the meals for her family.

Ramón Costa, his wife Sandra and their children, Lisandra (16) and Favio (6), live in Havana. Cuba is a tropical country so they eat a lot of fresh fruit – pineapples, watermelons, bananas, and papayas. Families in Cuba have ration books. These show how much food the family can buy every month.

Vocabulary | food and drink

1 Look at the photo and find these things.

orange juice ☐   cereal ☐   bananas ☐

carrots ☐   cola ☐   minced beef [A]   water ☐

Reading

2   **a** Read the text quickly and tick (✓) the countries it talks about.

Japan ☐   Britain ☐   Spain ☐   Cuba ☐
Russia ☐   United States ☐

b Read the text again and tick (✓) the correct answers.

Which family...	Ronayne	Ukita	Costa
1 eats a lot of fish?	☐	☐	☐
2 eats fresh fruit?	☐	☐	☐
3 has a ration book?	☐	☐	☐
4 eats at fast food restaurants?	☐	☐	☐
5 doesn't have time to cook?	☐	☐	☐
6 has dinner together?	☐	☐	☐

Grammar | countable and uncountable nouns

3   **a** Look at the picture and answer the questions.

1   Can you count the eggs?
2   Can you count the cereal?
3   Which is uncountable, *eggs* or *cereal*?

b Here is the Ronayne family shopping list. Answer the questions.

1 Choose the correct alternatives.

a The red words are *countable/ uncountable* nouns.

b The blue words are *countable/ uncountable* nouns.

c Uncountable nouns do not have *singular/plural* forms.

> 12 hot dogs
> 450g cereal
> 12 eggs
> 4 litres milk
> 2 litres orange juice
> 18 bananas
> 1 pizza
> 675g minced beef

2 How do we measure uncountable nouns?

c Write the headings in the Active grammar box.

Uncountable nouns   Countable nouns

Active grammar

1 _____

- They have singular and plural forms.
- We can use numbers in front of them.

2 _____

- They do not have plural forms.
- We cannot use numbers in front of them.
- We often use quantity words (e.g. *litres, kilos*) + *of* in front of them.

see Reference page 43

4 **a** Here are the shopping lists for the Costa and Ukita families. Write the food words in the table.

> **Costa**
> 1 pineapple
> 4kg bread
> 1kg pasta
> 2 watermelons
> 3 papayas
> 500g coffee
> 12 bananas
> 750g cereal

> **Ukita**
> 5kg rice
> 4 litres milk
> 2 pizzas
> 2kg tuna
> 12 eggs
> 300g beef
> 1 kg tomatoes
> 2 litres cola

COUNTABLE	UNCOUNTABLE
pineapple	bread

b Answer the questions, then complete the Active grammar box.

1 How much coffee does the Costa family buy each week?

2 How many pineapples do they buy?

Active grammar

We use *How* _____ with countable nouns.

We use *How* _____ with uncountable nouns.

see Reference page 43

5 **a** Complete with words and phrases from the box.

> 2kg   coffee   much   tomatoes   many   six

A: How (1) _____ rice do you buy each week?

B: I usually buy (2) _____ of rice.

A: And how many (3) _____ do you eat?

B: About (4) _____ .

A: How much (5) _____ do you buy?

B: I buy about 250g of coffee.

A: How (6) _____ pineapples do you get?

B: Oh, only one.

b **4.1** Listen and check your answers.

6 **4.2** Listen and complete the quantities.

6 litres water

1 _____ milk   4 _____ coffee

2 _____ rice   5 _____ cheese

3 _____ bananas

HOW TO … say quantities and numbers

Number	Quantity
201 *two hundred and one*	litres (l)
450 *four hundred and fifty*	grammes (g)
675 *six hundred and seventy-five*	kilos (kg)
1.5 *one point five/one and a half*	

7 Ask questions about your partner's weekly shopping. Make notes and tell the class.

A: *How much rice do you buy?*

B: *500 grammes./I don't buy rice.*

Vocabulary | containers

1   **a** Look at the advert and discuss the questions.

   1   What is the TV programme about?

   2   Who introduces the programme?

   3   Which food in the bins is healthy (good for you)? Which food is unhealthy (bad for you)?

   b Find examples of these containers in the bins. Use a dictionary to help you.

   > bag bottle box can carton packet

In the rubbish bin

People's rubbish tells us about their lives. Tonight Laurence Redburn looks at the diet of two families.

Tuesday 9.00p.m. Channel 6

Listening

2   **a** **4.3** Listen to the first part of the TV programme. Write A or B by the correct bin.

   b Listen again. Write the names of food and drink in the correct column.

HEALTHY FOOD	UNHEALTHY FOOD
vegetables	burgers
pasta	crisps

Person to person

3   Discuss.

   1   Do you agree with Laurence about the diets of the two families?

   2   What other food is healthy/ unhealthy, do you think?

   3   Tell your partner about your diet.

Grammar | *a/an, some* and *any*

4   Look at these sentences. Complete the Active grammar box with *a/an, some* or *any*.

   We have some cans... We have a bottle ...

   Do they eat any vegetables or any fruit? They eat some pasta ...

Active grammar

Noun	Singular countable	Plural countable	Uncountable
➕	_____	_____	_____
➖	*a/an*	*any*	*any*
❓	*a/an*	_____	*any*

see Reference page 43

5   **a** Complete the gaps with *a/an, some* or *any*.

   We don't have <u>any</u> potatoes.

   1   I want _____ potatoes and _____ carrots, please.

   2   Can I have _____ apple now?

   3   Can I have _____ bottle of water, please?

   4   I have _____ fruit here – do you want _____ banana?

   5   We don't eat _____ meat.

   b Correct the <u>underlined</u> mistakes in this paragraph.

   I like Italian food. Every Thursday evening we cook <u>a pasta</u> with <u>any minced beef</u> and <u>a tomatoes</u>. We have <u>some bottle</u> of water with the meal. We eat a lot of meat, but we don't eat <u>some chicken</u> – we don't like chicken. We also eat <u>any vegetables</u> every day.

Pronunciation

6 **a** **4.4** Listen to the vowel sounds in these words. Can you hear the difference?

/æ/	/ʌ/
pasta	some

b **4.5** Listen. <u>Underline</u> the /æ/ and /ʌ/ sounds. Then repeat the sentences.

1 He has lunch on Sundays in his club.
2 My family travels by taxi, but my young cousin takes the bus.
3 Anne and Sally have butter on their pasta.

Vocabulary | adjectives

7 **a** Match the pictures to the adjectives.

happy ☐   healthy ☐
hungry ☐   thirsty ☐
tired ☐   unhappy ☐
unhealthy ☐ fit ☐

b Which adjectives have a positive meaning? Which have a negative meaning?

Reading

A	B	C
Dear Laurence I'm always hungry. I eat three good meals a day but then I want crisps and biscuits too. Of course, now I'm quite fat! Can you help me? Lois	**Dear Laurence** I know I have an unhealthy diet. I work about ten hours a day and I get home late, so I don't have time to cook and I eat convenience food. What can I do? James	**Dear Laurence** I try to eat a good diet – I eat pasta and vegetables, and I don't eat any meat, fish or cheese – but I'm always tired. What's wrong with my diet? Karin

8 **a** Laurence also writes about diet in a magazine. Read the letters above and match them to the problems.

1 He/She doesn't have time to cook.
2 He/She eats a lot.
3 He/She feels tired all the time.

b Read Laurence's answer to one letter.

1 Which letter does it answer?
2 How does he start his answer?
3 How does he make the two suggestions?

> Dear _____
> It's horrible when you feel tired all the time. You need some meat, fish or cheese in your diet – they give you energy. Also, why don't you take some exercise? That gives you energy too. How about a walk every evening after work? I hope that helps.
>
> Laurence

Writing

9 **a** Read the other two letters again and look at Laurence's notes. Which notes are for which letter?

1 salads are quick and healthy *letter B*
2 eat fruit, not crisps and biscuits
3 go to the doctor
4 don't work ten hours a day
5 some food is quick to cook, e.g. fresh pasta
6 eat only small meals

b Make more suggestions for the writers of the two letters.

c In pairs, write an answer to one of the other letters.

1 Think of two or three suggestions.
2 Start the letter, write your suggestions and finish the letter.
3 Give your letter to another pair to correct and improve it.

Listening

1 Discuss.

   1 Where is the place in the photo?

   2 Do you eat at places like these? Which places?

2 **a** **4.6** Listen to a dialogue in a fast food restaurant. Who orders these things? Write J for Jenny and S for Sam.

   cheese sandwich ☐

   fries ☐   salad ☐

   coffee ☐   water ☐

   b Listen again and complete the bill below (1–4).

🍴 Restaurant

```
================================
Cheese sandwich          x1  $4.50
Large (1) _____       x1  $3.00
(2)_____ salad        x1  $4.00
(3)_____ coffee       x1  $2.95
Small mineral (4)_____    x1  $2.25

TOTAL                     $ (5)_____
Service & tax included
```

3 **a** **4.7** Listen and complete number 5 in Ex. 2b.

   b Listen again and answer the questions.

   1 What does Jenny really like?

   2 How does Sam ask for the price of the meal?

   3 How does Sam pay for the meal?

4 **a** This is the menu from the fast food restaurant. Match the headings to A–C.

   Drinks   Main dishes   Side orders

A _____		B _____		C _____	
Sandwiches		**Regular fries**	$___	**Regular coffee**	$___
Cheese	$___	**Large fries**	$___	**Large coffee**	$___
Chicken salad	$___	**Small salad**	$___	**Orange juice**	$___
Tuna and mayonnaise	$___	**Medium salad**	$___	**Regular cola**	$___
(choose from white or brown bread)		**Large salad**	$___	**Large cola**	$___
Burgers and pizzas				**Small mineral water**	$___
Burger	$___			**Large mineral water**	$___
Vegetarian pizza	$___				
Chicken piece	$___				

b Work in pairs.

Student A: turn to page 125.

Student B: ask your partner questions to complete the menu.

How much is a burger?

Grammar | object pronouns

5 **a** **4.8** Listen and complete the sentences.

1 OK. A large cup of coffee for _____ and a small glass of mineral water for _____.

2 No, that's not for _____.

3 Two vegetarian pizzas? I really like _____!

4 A medium salad for _____, sir.

5 Oh no, the salad's for _____.

b Look at the tapescript on page 153 and check your answers. Use the information to complete the Active grammar box.

Active grammar

Subject pronouns	Object pronouns
I	_me_
he	_____
she	_____
it	_it_
we	_____
you	_____
they	_____

see Reference page 43

6 Tell the waitress. Complete the sentences with object pronouns.

Well, who is this for?

you: 'It isn't for _me_.'

1 your boyfriend: 'It isn't for _____.'

2 your mother: 'It isn't for _____.'

3 you and your friend: 'It isn't for _____.'

4 your brother and sister: 'It isn't for _____.'

7 **a** Match 1–7 to a–g.

1	What	a	much is that?
2	I'd like	b	pay by credit card?
3	Jenny, what would	c	can I get you today?
4	Do you	d	a cheese sandwich, please.
5	Sam, do	e	have salads?
6	How	f	you like?
7	Can I	g	you want some juice?

b Look at the tapescripts on page 153 and check your answers. Then complete the sentences in the How to box.

HOW TO …

order in a fast food restaurant

Ask questions	_____ you have salads?
Say what you want	I'd _____ a cheese sandwich, please.
Ask about prices	How _____ is that?

c Use some of the words from Ex. 7a to complete this dialogue.

A: Hello, what _____ I get you today?

B: _____ like a vegetarian burger, please.

A: Any side orders?

B: _____ you have salads?

A: No, we don't. Do you _____ fries?

B: OK. Small fries.

A: Anything to drink?

B: Yes, I'd _____ an orange juice, please.

A: OK.

B: How _____ is that?

A: That's €10.95.

B: _____ I pay by credit card?

Speaking

8 Work in groups of three. Use the menu in Ex. 4a.

Student A: you are a waiter/waitress. Take the customers' order.

Students B and C: you are customers at the restaurant. Look at the menu, choose the things you want and order a meal.

4 Communication

Shopping at a market

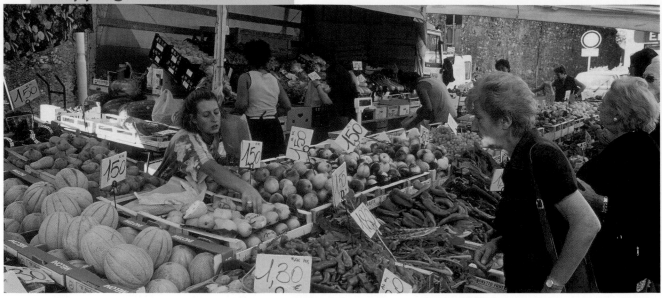

1 **a** [4.9] Listen. What does the woman ask for? Tick (✓) the blue boxes.

apples ☐ ☐ carrots ☐ ☐ tomatoes ☐ ☐
bananas ☐ ☐ chicken ☐ ☐ potatoes ☐ ☐
beef ☐ ☐ melon ☐ ☐ tuna ☐ ☐

b Listen again. What things can she buy? Tick (✓) the red boxes.

c How much does the woman pay for all her shopping? Listen and check if necessary.

2 **a** [4.10] Listen to the intonation. Write ↗ if it goes up and ↘ if it goes down.

I'd like three bananas ↗, a kilo of apples ☐ and a melon ☐.
I'd like 500g of minced beef ☐, 200g of tuna ☐ and a chicken ☐.

b Listen again and repeat.

c Play a game in groups. Choose food and drink from the box below. Follow the example, and be careful to use the correct intonation. How long can you continue?

> minced beef   chicken   fish   lamb   tuna
> butter   cheese   eggs   milk   pasta   apples
> ice cream   bananas   carrots   melons
> papayas   pineapples   potatoes   tomatoes
> coffee   cola   orange juice   tea   water

Student A: *I'd like some coffee.*

Student B: *I'd like some coffee and a bottle of water.*

Student C: *I'd like some coffee, a bottle of water and three apples.*

Student D: *I'd like some coffee, a bottle of water, three apples and ...*

3 **a** Half the class are shoppers at a market. The other half are shop assistants. Read your roles.

b When you finish, tell the class about the things you have.

Shoppers

Work in pairs. Choose six things from the box in Ex. 2c and write your shopping list. You have 25 euros for all your shopping. Look at the tapescript on page 153 and prepare to go shopping. Ask the shop assistants and try to buy all your items. How much do you pay?

Shop assistants

1   Your teacher gives you a letter, A, B, C or D.
A: you sell fruit and vegetables.
B: you sell drinks.
C: you sell meat and fish.
D: you sell dairy food (butter, milk, etc.).

2   Look at the box in Ex. 2c and the list on page 43 and find the correct type of food for your shop. Choose four items and write them down. Write a price next to each item, e.g. *coffee – 3 euros for 250 g, water – 1 euro a bottle.*

3   Look at the tapescript on page 153 and prepare to answer your customers' questions.

Countable and uncountable nouns; *How much?/How many?*

Countable nouns are things that we can count. They have singular and plural forms and we can use numbers in front of them.

one banana   three bananas   twenty-five bananas

Use *How many ...?* to ask questions about the number of countable nouns.

How many *bananas do you buy every week?*

Uncountable nouns are things we can't count. They do not have plural forms and we cannot use numbers in front of them.

Use *How much ...?* to ask questions about the quantity of uncountable nouns.

How much *water do you drink every day?*

Show the quantity *(how much/many)* of countable and uncountable nouns by using another noun (e.g. *a bag*) or a measurement (e.g. *kilos*) + *of* in front of the noun.

A bag *of bananas.* ***Half a kilo*** *of bananas.*
A glass *of water.* ***A litre*** *of water.*

a/an, some and *any*

Singular countable nouns

Use *a/an* before singular countable nouns when there is only one of the noun. Use *a/an* in positive and negative statements and in questions.

⊕	*We have a car.*
⊖	*We don't have a car.*
?	*Do you have a car?*

Plural countable nouns

Use *some* and *any* to talk about a number of something, when we don't know how many, or the number isn't important. We usually use *some* in positive statements, and *any* in negative statements and questions. Use *some* and *any* with plural countable nouns.

⊕	*We have some magazines.*
⊖	*We don't have any magazines.*
?	*Do you have any magazines?*

Uncountable nouns

We also use *some* and *any* with uncountable nouns.

⊕	*We have some cheese.*
⊖	*We don't have any cheese.*
?	*Do you have any cheese?*

Object pronouns

Use subject pronouns (see page 13) before verbs and object pronouns after verbs.

Subject pronouns		Object pronouns	
	I		*me*
	he		*him*
	she		*her*
	it		*it*
	we		*us*
	you		*you*
	they		*them*

*He loves **her**.*

*He loves **them**.*

*She loves **him**.*

*They love **me**!*

Key vocabulary

Food

Dishes: burger fries pizza salad sandwich

Meat and fish: (minced) beef chicken lamb trout tuna

Dairy: butter cheese cream ice cream milk

Fruit and vegetables: apple banana carrot papaya pineapple potato tomato (water)melon

Drinks: coffee cola fruit/orange juice tea milk water

Other: biscuits (white/brown) bread cereal crisps eggs mayonnaise pasta rice sugar

Money

cheque coin credit card note receipt

Adjectives for physical and emotional states

fit happy/unhappy healthy/unhealthy hungry thirsty tired

1 Match the sentence halves.

1 I usually buy a   a tuna for this recipe.
2 We often get ten   b of chocolates to his girlfriend every Saturday.
3 She puts 100g
4 I drink a carton   c of milk every day.
5 We need a can of   d pizza on Friday evening.
6 He takes a box   e bags of crisps at the supermarket.
    f of cheese in the omelette.

2 Choose the correct alternatives.

How *much*/*many* oranges do you eat?

1 How *much*/*many* students come to your lesson?
2 She drinks three litres of *waters*/*water* every day.
3 Let's have *2/2kg* of those nice brown eggs for breakfast.
4 How *much*/*many* money do you have in your pocket?
5 How *many*/*much* sugar do you eat every week?

3 Amanda phones her husband, but he doesn't answer. Complete her message with *a*, *some* or *any*.

Hello John. Oh, no, it's a message. He isn't there. Mmm. John, please listen to this message. Can you go to the shops and get _some_ things for dinner? We need (1) _____ fish, and (2) _____ box of eggs. Mmm, I think we have (3) _____ potatoes, but we don't have (4) _____ onions. Do we have (5) _____ carrots? Can you check? Please buy (6) _____ cheese, and I'd like (7) _____ carton of orange juice. That's it. Oh ... we don't have (8) _____ butter – can you get some? Thanks. See you later.

4 Replace the words in brackets ( ) with the correct pronouns and rewrite the sentences.

(Mr Bosgrove) takes (my friend and me) to work in his car.

He takes us to work in his car.

1 (My mother and I) go shopping with (Julia and Carla) every Saturday.
2 (My sister) gets up before (my brother and me).
3 (David and Serena) don't take (the children) on holiday.
4 (My uncle) uses (the computer) every day.
5 (My friend and I) have lunch with (Maria) every Tuesday.

5 Complete the dialogue with the correct pronouns.

A: Hello, Mrs Lovett. How are _you_ ?
B: Oh, hello Sonia. (1) _____'m fine thanks.
A: How's your husband?
B: (2) _____'s fine. He works in the supermarket now.
A: Yes, I know. I see (3) _____ when I do my shopping. And how are the twins, Jake and Jerry?
B: Oh, (4) _____ are very well.
A: Do they go to school on the bus?
B: No. I take (5) _____ with (6) _____ in the car every morning.
A: Who is their teacher?
B: It's Mrs Moore. Do you know (7)_____?
A: Yes, I do. (8) _____ lives in our street. She always says 'Hello' to (9) _____.

6 **a** Put the letters in the correct order to write the food words.

nseyaimaon   m_ayonnaise_

1 ntau   t_____
2 errbug   b_____
3 eabrd   b_____
4 onermwalte   w_____
5 otmotsea   t_____
6 ckechin   c_____
7 ilmk   m_____
8 apzzi   p_____
9 crie   r_____

b Circle the odd-one-out.

coffee tea (rice) water

1 beef chicken trout lamb
2 apple fries tomato carrot
3 butter ice cream milk sugar
4 sandwich coffee tea water

5 Home

B

C

D

Lead-in

1 a Which rooms from the box can you see in the photos?

bathroom   bedroom   dining room   garden   garage
kitchen   living room

b **5.1** Where can you do these activities? Match the places in the box to the activities. Then listen and check.

sunbathe *You can sunbathe in the garden.*

1 cook   2 sleep   3 have a shower   4 put your car
5 eat   6 watch TV

2 a **5.2** Tick (✓) the landscapes in the photos. Listen and check.

a beach ☐   mountains ☐   a river ☐   a forest ☐   a city ☐
a lake ☐   a desert ☐   the sea ☐

b Which other words for landscapes do you know? Make a list.

c Answer the questions.

1 What is in the north of your country?
(the centre/the south/the west/the east)
2 What can you see from your living room window?
(bedroom window/kitchen window)

3 Play a game in groups. Think of a country and describe its landscape. Can other students guess the country?

This country has beaches in the north. It has a big city in the east, mountains in the south and a famous forest in the south-west.

Reading

1 What kind of home do you live in? Do you like your home? Why/Why not?

2 **a** Look at the text quickly and answer the questions.

1 Where is this text from?
2 What is unusual about the homes in the text?

b Read the text. Mark true (T) or false (F).

1 The ship has:
   a 110 apartments. ☐
   b six restaurants. ☐
   c two swimming pools. ☐
   d two gyms. ☐
2 The apartments have:
   a a large living room. ☐
   b a dining room. ☐
   c a garden. ☐
   d a private terrace. ☐

The World of ResidenSea

Own a private luxury home ... at sea!

There are 110 luxury apartments on our ship The World, but that's not all! There are four restaurants, two swimming pools and a gym. There are shops, but there aren't any factories or cars, so there's no city stress. All our apartments have a large living room (with dining area) and two or three bedrooms. Each bedroom has a private bathroom and there's a cooker, a fridge, a dishwasher and a microwave in each well-equipped kitchen. Of course, there isn't a garden but each apartment has a private terrace. All the living rooms have modern TV, DVD and CD players. Choose from four different styles for your sofas, chairs, beds and other furniture, and make your apartment on the ship a very comfortable home.

—————————————— The World of ResidenSea ——————————————

Vocabulary | equipment and furniture

3 **a** Look at the floor plan. Label the rooms and the furniture.

b Write the headings in the table. Then write two or three more things by each heading.

> furniture   kitchen equipment   ~~rooms~~
> living room equipment   ship's facilities

1	_rooms_	kitchen
2	_____	cupboard
3	_____	fridge
4	_____	TV
5	_____	swimming pools

Lifelong learning

Personalise it!
When you want to learn new words, it is useful to write them in a personal sentence.
fridge – *My fridge is very old – it's useless!*
cupboard – *I have a big cupboard in my bedroom.*

Grammar | *there is/there are*

4 Complete the Active grammar box with *'s, is, isn't, are* or *aren't*.

Active grammar

	Singular	Plural
+	There*'s* a gym. (There *is*)	There _____ 110 apartments.
−	There _____ a garden.	There _____ any cars.
?	_____ there a bookshop?	_____ there any music shops?
	Yes, there is. No, there _____.	Yes, there _____. No, there aren't.

see Reference page 53

5 Look at the text and the floor plan again. Complete the sentences with *'s, is, are, isn't* or *aren't*.

1 There _____ some shops on the ship, but there _____ any cars.
2 _____ there any factories? No, there _____.
3 There _____ a terrace in each apartment.
4 _____ there a dining room? No, there _____.

6 **a** Look at Ex. 2b. Make sentences.

There are 110 luxury apartments on the ship.
There aren't six restaurants.

b Ask and answer about the floor plan.

A: *Is there a bath in the apartment?*
B: *There's a bath in bedroom one, but there isn't a bath in bedroom two.*

7 Tell your partner about your home.

There are three bedrooms in my apartment but there's only one bathroom.

Listening

8 **a** `5.3` Jon Nott wants to buy an apartment on the ship. Listen and answer the questions.

1 What is Jon interested in?
2 Are there two-bedroom or three-bedroom apartments for sale?
3 What is the price of an apartment with two bedrooms?
4 Does Jon think the apartment is expensive?
5 Do you think he has the money for the apartment?

b Listen again. Number Jon's questions in the correct order. Then answer them.

1 How many bathrooms are there? ☐
2 Can I ask you some questions? ☐
3 How much space is there? ☐
4 Are there any apartments for sale now? ☐
5 How much does the apartment cost? ☐
6 How many bedrooms are there? ☐

Speaking

9 Work in pairs.

Student A: read the information below.
Student B: look at the information on page 126.

Student A

You are interested in a town house. Student B has the details. Ask questions to find out these things about the house:

1 how big?
2 how many rooms?
3 what rooms?
4 garden/terrace?
5 where?
6 price?

Do you want to buy the house?

Now answer Student B's questions about the house below.

beautiful country cottage
- 120 square metres
- three bedrooms, two bathrooms
- living room, dining room
- kitchen/breakfast room
- two large gardens, front and back
- two kilometres from village with shops

€240,000

Grammar	*have got*
Can do	ask and talk about important possessions

Vocabulary | possessions

1   **a** In pairs, look at the four rooms. Which room(s) do you like? Why?

b What's in the pictures? You have three minutes. Make a list of all the things you can see.

tables, cooker, mobile phone

c Close your books. In pairs, try to remember the things in the pictures.

There's a sofa in every room.
There's a plant in one room ...

Listening

2   **a** `5.4` Amanda Myers asks Pete Morgan some questions. Listen. Which picture shows Pete's flat?

b Listen again. Tick (✓) the things Pete has got and cross (✗) the things he hasn't got.

studio apartment ☐   house ☐   garden ☐   terrace ☐   fridge ☐
cooker ☐   sink ☐   microwave ☐   coffee table ☐   chairs ☐
sofa ☐   dining table ☐   TV ☐   music system ☐   laptop computer ☐
mobile phone ☐

Grammar | *have got*

3   **a** `5.5` Listen to the first part of the dialogue again and complete the gaps.

Amanda: Have you _____ your own house?

Pete: No, I _____. I _____ got a modern studio apartment in the centre of town.

Amanda: _____ it got a garden?

Pete: No, it _____ got a garden, but it _____ got a small terrace.

b Complete the Active grammar box.

Active grammar

+	I/We/You/They	_____	got
	He/She/It	_'s_	
−	_____	haven't	got
	He/She/It	_____	
?	_____	I/we/you/they	got ...?
	_____	he/she/it	
	Yes, No,	I/we/you/they	_have_. _____.
	Yes, No,	he/she/it	has. hasn't.

see Reference page 53

4 **a** Find the false sentences and correct them.

He's got a house.   ✗   *He hasn't got a house.*

1 He's got an apartment in the centre of town.
2 It hasn't got a kitchen.
3 He's got a laptop computer.
4 He hasn't got a dining table.
5 He hasn't got any chairs.
6 He's got a garden.

b Make questions from the prompts and write <u>true</u> short answers.

London/five airports?

Has London got five airports? Yes, it has.

1 your town/a theatre?
2 your parents/a car?
3 you/a computer?
4 your teacher/any pens?

Pronunciation

5 **a** `5.6` Listen to the <u>underlined</u> sounds. Which sound is different?

He's g<u>o</u>t a l<u>a</u>pt<u>o</u>p, a c<u>a</u>t and a w<u>a</u>tch.

b `5.7` Listen and tick (✓) the word you hear.

1	hot	☐	hat	☐
2	on	☐	an	☐
3	top	☐	tap	☐
4	pocket	☐	packet	☐

Speaking

6 Work in pairs to describe rooms.

Student A: choose one of the rooms from Ex. 1 but don't tell your partner. Talk about your room. Use *there is/are* and *have got*.

Student B: listen to your partner. Ask questions. Which room is it?

7 **a** Make a list of your family members and important personal possessions. Use the ideas in the box.

Family: husband, two children
Accommodation: two-bedroom apartment
Furniture: desk
Electrical equipment: CD player
Pets: cat
Transport: bicycle
Other: Swiss watch

b In pairs, find four things that ...

- your partner has got but you haven't got.

1 _____ 2 _____ 3 _____ 4 _____

- you've got but your partner hasn't got.

1 _____ 2 _____ 3 _____ 4 _____

A: *Have you got a car?*
B: *No, I haven't but I've got a motorbike.*

Writing

8 Write a paragraph about where your partner lives and the things he/she has and hasn't got. Use the How to box to help you.

Mariela lives in a house with a garden. She's got two sisters. She's got a computer and a printer but she hasn't got a mobile phone.

HOW TO ... add information

Use *and* to join similar sentences or parts of sentences.
He's got a mobile phone. He's got a TV. =
He's got a mobile phone and a TV.

Use *but* to give different/contrasting information.
I've got a house. I haven't got a car. =
I've got a house but I haven't got a car.

5.3 | World class

Grammar	modifiers *(very, quite, really)*
Can do	write an informal email about your country

Listening

1 **a** Match these places to the photos. You don't need one word.

mountain ☐ desert ☐ forest ☐ city ☐ river ☐ lake ☐

b Work with a partner. In which countries are the places in the photos?

2 **5.8** Listen to five people talking about their homes and check your answers to Ex. 1a and Ex. 1b.

3 **a** Listen again. Make notes about the places in the table.

PLACE	LANDSCAPE	WHICH PART?
1 *Spain*	_____	_____
2 _____	_____	*south*
3 _____	*beautiful lakes*	_____
4 *Kefallonia*	_____	_____
5 _____	_____	*west*

b Make sentences about the places with *There's* or *There are*.

There's a famous desert in the south of Spain.

Grammar | modifiers

4 **a** **5.9** Listen and complete the sentences with *quite, really, very* or *not very*.

1 It's _____ hot and dry.
2 The south is _____ cold.
3 It's _____ popular now with people from other countries.
4 It's _____ busy and noisy, and it's _____ friendly.

b Write the correct modifiers next to the thermometer.

_____ hot, _____ hot
hot
_____ hot
_____ hot

see Reference page 53

5 Make sentences.

Russia/big *Russia is very big.*

1 New Zealand/big
2 Mount Everest/high
3 The Pyrenees/high
4 Mexico City/busy
5 Canada/cold
6 Britain/cold

Vocabulary | adjectives to describe places

6 **a** Which adjectives can we use with *desert*? Look at the word map and add two adjectives from the box.

hot — desert

| beautiful busy cold dry |
| famous green high hot |
| huge noisy popular |

b Make word maps for *mountain, island, forest, beach* and *city*.

Pronunciation

7 **a** **5.10** Listen and answer the questions.

river   desert

1   How many syllables do the words have?
2   Is the second syllable strong or weak?

Lifelong learning

Use your dictionary ...

to find how many syllables there are in a word.

two: moun•tain three: mic•ro•wave

---

b **5.11** Look at the words in the box. Mark the syllables and <u>underline</u> the strong syllable.

<u>riv</u>/er <u>des</u>/ert

centre island Japan Poland China

c Listen and check your answers.

Speaking

8 **a** Write answers to these questions. Use the How to box to help you.

1   Where do you live?
2   What kind of landscape is there in your country? Where is it?
3   Which parts of your country do you like/not like?

HOW TO ...	**describe where you live**	
	Say where you live	*I'm from ... I live in ...*
	Describe the landscape	*There are ... in the south/north of ...*
	Give your opinion	*I like/don't like ... because ...*

b In pairs use your answers to describe where you live and your country. Then describe where a friend lives, or another country.

Writing

9 **a** Read the email and answer the questions.

Are there mountains in Australia?

Yes, there are. They're in the south.

1   What is there in the north of Australia?
2   Where are the deserts in Australia?
3   Is there a big city in the west?
4   Where are the famous beaches?

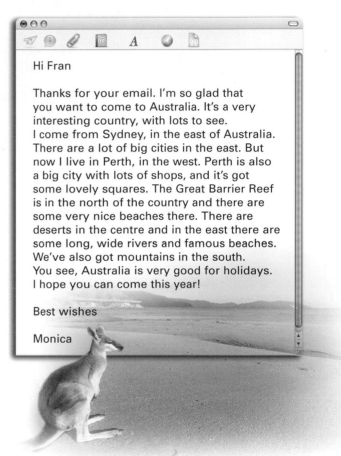

Hi Fran

Thanks for your email. I'm so glad that you want to come to Australia. It's a very interesting country, with lots to see. I come from Sydney, in the east of Australia. There are a lot of big cities in the east. But now I live in Perth, in the west. Perth is also a big city with lots of shops, and it's got some lovely squares. The Great Barrier Reef is in the north of the country and there are some very nice beaches there. There are deserts in the centre and in the east there are some long, wide rivers and famous beaches. We've also got mountains in the south. You see, Australia is very good for holidays. I hope you can come this year!

Best wishes

Monica

b Match these expressions from the email to their purpose.

1   Hi Fran   a   opening sentence
2   Thanks for your email.   b   closing sentence
3   I hope you can   c   starting the email
    come this year!   (greeting)
4   Best wishes   d   ending the email

10 Write an email to a friend about your country.

1   Look at your answers to Ex. 8a. Which information do you want to put in the email?
2   Use *and* and *but* to join sentences.
3   In groups, read each other's emails. Add to the information if possible.

Furnishing an apartment

1 Look at the photo. What has the apartment got? What hasn't it got?

2 **a** This is your new apartment. What do you think you need? Use a dictionary and choose ten things.

armchair ☐ bed ☐ bookshelves ☐
CD player ☐ coffee machine ☐ computer ☐
cupboard ☐ desk ☐ dining table and chairs ☐
DVD player ☐ lamp ☐ microwave ☐
phone with answering machine ☐ sofa ☐
television ☐ vacuum cleaner ☐ video ☐
washing machine ☐

b Compare your list with a partner. Agree on ten important things and put the things in order 1–10 (1 = very useful, 10 = not very useful).

3 **a** Work in groups of three. You can buy things for your apartment but you've only got €1,000!

You each have information from a different place. You can talk about your information but you can't show it to your partners. Talk about the things you want for your apartment, compare the prices and complete the shopping list of the things you want to buy and their cost. Remember you only have €1,000!

Are there any sofas in your list?

How much do they cost?

What have we got now?

NEW APARTMENT SHOPPING LIST

ITEM	SUPPLIER	COST
lamp	Furnishyourapartment.com	€45

Student A: you have information from the Internet. Turn to page 126.

Student B: you have a catalogue. Turn to page 129.

Student C: you have information from a local shop. Look at the bottom of this page.

b When you finish, compare your list with other groups.

Student C: you have this information from a local shop.

Davis Electrical
Today's bargains!

Home cinema
(DVD and flatscreen TV)

Only ų600!

Combination DVD player and TV

ų225

Japanese large TV and video combination

ų400

Washing machine

ų330

Vacuum cleaner

ų125

CD player

ų195

Digital phone and answering machine

ų130

Italian coffee machine

ų150

there is/there are

	Singular	Plural
+	There's ... (There is)	There are ...
−	There isn't ... (There is not)	There aren't ... (There are not)
?	Is there ...?	Are there ...?
	Yes, there is./ No, there isn't.	Yes, there are./ No, there aren't.

Use *there is* (+ a singular noun) and *there are* (+ a plural noun) to talk about people or things for the first time. We often use them to describe places.

Use *there's*, *there isn't* and *there aren't* when you speak.

There's a huge forest in the west.

Use *There's*, not *There are*, to introduce a list of singular objects.

There's a swimming pool, a lake and a restaurant at the holiday village.

have got

	I/We/You/They	He/She/It
+	've got (have got)	's got (has got)
−	haven't got (have not got)	hasn't got (has not got)
?	Have ... got?	Has ... got?
	Yes, we have. No, I haven't.	Yes, it has. No, she hasn't.

We usually use the contracted forms: *'s got ...*, *'ve got ...*, *hasn't got ...*, *haven't got ...*

There are no contracted forms for questions.

Have you got a DVD player?

We often use short answers when we answer *have got* questions.

A: *Have you got a television?*
B: *Yes, I have./No, I haven't.*

Use *have got* to talk about our possessions and family/friends. Don't use *have got* in very formal English.

I've got a sports car.
They've got two sisters.

Modifiers

The words *(not) very*, *quite* and *really* are modifiers. We put them in front of an adjective to make it stronger or weaker. Use *very* and *really* to make the adjective stronger.

*This car is **very/really** expensive!*

Use *quite* or *not very* to make the adjective weaker.

*This car is **quite** expensive.*
*This car is**n't very** expensive.*

Adjectives and places

Use adjectives to describe nouns. These adjectives describe places:

a hot, dry desert
a busy, noisy city
a long, wide river
a beautiful lake
a high mountain
a lovely beach
a green forest
a popular island

We usually put adjectives in front of the noun. We often put a comma between two adjectives in front of a noun.

Key vocabulary

Types of home
house   apartment   studio
cottage   town house

Rooms and parts of a house
bathroom   bedroom
dining room   garden   garage
hall   living room   roof terrace
terrace

Furniture
armchair   bed   bookshelves
chair   coffee table   cupboard
desk   dining chairs/table   sofa
table

Equipment and possessions
answering machine   bath
CD player   coffee machine
cooker   dishwasher
DVD player   fridge   microwave
MP3 player   music system
shower   sink   toilet
vacuum cleaner   video
washing machine

1 Look at the floor plan and complete the dialogue with *there is* or *there are*.

A: Good morning. Can you give me some information about the apartment on Chandos Road?

B: Yes, of course. It's a very nice, big apartment. (1) *There are* three bedrooms, ...

A: (2) _____ a bathroom with each bedroom?

B: No, (3) _____ . The main bedroom has got a bathroom, and then (4) _____ one other bathroom in the apartment.

A: OK. Is the kitchen big?

B: Yes, it is, and it's got a lot of equipment.

A: What about the dining room?

B: Ah, well, (5) _____ a dining room. But (6) _____ a large living room with a dining area.

A: I know there's a garden but (7) _____ any terraces?

B: No, (8) _____, I'm afraid.

A: And finally, (9) _____ a garage?

B: Yes, (10) _____ a garage at the front of the house.

2 Write negative sentences.

We've got an apartment in London.

We haven't got an apartment in London.

1 I've got a video camera.
2 She's got a mobile phone.
3 They've got a lot of money.
4 Their car's got a CD player.
5 England's got a lot of mountains.

3 Write questions and short answers.

Simon/sports car? No, _____.

Has Simon got a sports car? No, *he hasn't.*

1 Rachel/laptop computer? Yes, _____.
2 they/big house? No, _____.
3 your flat/garden? No, _____.
4 Kelly/washing machine? Yes, _____.
5 Spain/king? Yes, _____.

4 Complete the sentences with modifiers. You choose the modifier.

English is *quite* easy to learn.

1 My town/city is _____ beautiful.
2 People in my country are _____ friendly.
3 My country is _____ popular with tourists.
4 My diet is _____ healthy.
5 My home is _____ noisy.

5 Match the words in the box to the places on the map (A–I).

> a beach   a city   a desert   a forest   an island
> a lake   mountains   a river   the sea

6 Write the things from the box in the rooms where you usually find them. Some things can go in two or three rooms.

> armchair   bed   bookshelves   CD player
> coffee table   cooker   cupboard   dishwasher
> fridge   sofa   table   washing machine

6 City life

Lead-in

1 a Look at the photos. Which places in the box can you see?

> art gallery   bank   bar   bookshop   café   church   cinema
> factory   hospital   library   museum   newsagent's
> phone shop   police station   post office   restaurant   school
> square   supermarket   train station

b 6.1 Listen to the words from Ex. 1a. How many syllables does each word or phrase have? Practise saying the words.

art/gal/le/ry – 4   bank – 1

c What can you do in these places?

A: *What can you do in a bookshop?*

B: *You can buy books in a bookshop.*

2 a 6.2 Listen and complete the directions.

Turn *left* at the bookshop.

1 _____ straight on to the post office.

2 The bank is _____ the right.

3 _____ right at the church.

4 _____ along the road next to the park.

5 The school is on the _____.

b Match the directions to the diagrams.

6.1 | Changes

Grammar	past of *to be*: all forms; Past Simple of regular verbs: positive
Can do	talk about your past

Reading

1 **a** What are the buildings in the photos? Read the text and check your answers.

b Match the buildings with *now* and *in the past*.

		Now	In the past
1	The Hoover Building	an office	a hospital
2	The Musée d'Orsay	a supermarket	a train station
3	The Reina Sofía	an art gallery	a school
4	The Smolny Institute	a museum and art gallery	a factory

Grammar | past of *to be*

2 Choose the correct words in the rules in the Active grammar box, then complete the table in the Active grammar box.

Active grammar

We use *is* and *are* with *now/the past*.
We use *was* and *were* with *now/the past*.

	I/He/She/It	We/You/They
➕	was	_____
➖	_____	weren't
❓	_____ I/he/she/it?	Were we/you/they?
	Yes, I/he/she/it was.	Yes, we/you/they _____.
	No, I/he/she/it _____.	No, we/you/they weren't.

see Reference page 63

Changing **buildings**

You live in an apartment now, but was it an apartment fifty years ago? Maybe it wasn't an apartment, but a school or a factory …

The Hoover Building in London is a famous building from the 1930s. It was the main office and factory of the Hoover Company. It is now a supermarket.

The Musée d'Orsay in Paris was a train station in the early twentieth century. It is now an art gallery.

The Reina Sofía building was a hospital. It is now one of Madrid's main museums and art galleries.

The Smolny Institute in St Petersburg is now the office of the Governor of the city. It was a school for rich girls in the nineteenth century. The offices were classrooms.

3 Make two true sentences about each building.

The Hoover Building was a factory. It is now a supermarket.

Person to person

4 Where were you at these times? Ask and answer.

> ten minutes ago   an hour ago
> ~~six hours ago~~   yesterday at midday
> at eight o'clock last night
> last Sunday afternoon
> last Saturday evening

A: *Where were you six hours ago?*

B: *I was at home.*

A: *Were you in the living room?*

B: *No, I wasn't. I was in bed.*

Listening

5 **a** `6.3` Listen to four speakers. Which of the buildings in the photos does each speaker talk about?

Speaker 1 _____

Speaker 2 _____

Speaker 3 _____

Speaker 4 _____

b Look at this summary and find one new piece of information about each building.

The Hoover Building was a factory and offices: some people (1) _____ in the factory. They produced electrical equipment. Other people worked in the offices.

Doctors and nurses lived and worked in the San Carlos Hospital. They (2) _____ after sick people. The museum now has Picasso's *Guernica*.

Young women studied in the school. It (3) _____ into Lenin's main offices when he (4) _____ to come here in 1917, and he planned the Revolution here.

The Musée d'Orsay was a train station. It (5) _____ in 1900 but it (6) _____ in 1937. The museum opened in 1986, and France's Impressionist collection (7) _____ there.

Grammar | Past Simple of regular verbs (positive)

6 **a** Find the Past Simple of these verbs in the summary in Ex. 5b.

live _____   work _____   study _____
plan _____   open _____

b Match the verbs in Ex. 6a with these Past Simple endings. Then check in the Reference on page 63.

1   + -ed   3   + n + -ed
2   –y + -ied   4   + -d

c Complete gaps 1–7 in Ex. 5b with suitable verbs. Listen again to check.

7 Make sentences in the Past Simple from the prompts.

Doctors/work/in the San Carlos hospital

Doctors worked in the San Carlos hospital.

1   The Hoover Factory/produce/vacuum cleaners
2   Alicia/study/at the Sorbonne
3   My brother/start/a new job yesterday
4   My mother/marry/my father in 1977
5   That church/change/to apartments in 2002

Pronunciation

8 **a** `6.4` Listen to the Past Simple endings of these verbs. Are they all the same?

/t/   /d/   /ɪd/
work<u>ed</u>   open<u>ed</u>   decid<u>ed</u>

b `6.5` Listen and write the verbs in the correct column. Then repeat them.

visited finished lived changed started
looked produced planned studied

/t/ worked	/d/ opened	/ɪd/ decided

c Read a sentence from Ex. 7. Your partner listens and checks your pronunciation.

Speaking

9 Use the verbs from this lesson to make notes about your past. Tell your partner about your past.

When I was a child, we lived in Biarritz, but we moved in 1990 to Marseille.

Reading

1 Read the text and answer the questions.

   1 How many hours was Robin Andrews away from home?

   2 What does *missing* mean?

   3 Why is Robin confused?

2 **a** **6.6** Listen to an interview with Robin and answer the questions.

   1 Where was Robin the next morning?

   2 Who helped him?

   3 Who collected him?

b There are some mistakes in the interviewer's notes for her article. Listen and correct the underlined phrases.

   1 Robin disappeared <u>at 2.30</u>.

   2 He walked <u>three</u> kilometres to the village.

   3 He called <u>at the post office</u>.

   4 He wanted to go <u>to the bar</u>.

   5 <u>A young man</u> helped him.

   6 <u>His mother</u> collected him.

Vocabulary | prepositions of place

3 **a** Listen to the dialogue again. Tick (✓) the phrases you hear.

in the bank ☐
next to the supermarket ☐
at the phone shop ☐
to the Internet café ☐
in front of a library ☐
on the ground ☐
behind the police station ☐
at the bus station ☐
under the bridge ☐
between the trees ☐

b **6.7** Listen to the phrases in Ex. 3a and repeat them.

Man goes missing for 16 hours

Robin Andrews, 24, of Loxton Close, Shelton, was missing for sixteen hours last Tuesday. Mr Andrews disappeared at 2.30 in the afternoon when he walked out of the house to get some things in the village. In the village centre, three kilometres from his home, Mr Andrews collected some money from the cashpoint and called at the post office, but he doesn't remember anything after that. Mr Andrews is very confused, 'I wanted to go to the bar but something strange happened.' It seems that Mr Andrews arrived in Marbury, eight kilometres from Shelton, where ...

Lifelong learning

Words and pictures

Pictures can sometimes help you to learn words, like the diagrams of prepositions below.

4 Write the correct preposition under the diagrams.

Grammar | Past simple: questions

5 Read the questions in the Active grammar box and complete the rule. Choose the correct words

> ### Active grammar
>
> 1 *Did you get lost?*
>
> 2 *Where did you go then?*
>
> 3 *Did you go to sleep?*
>
> To make questions in the Past Simple, use *do/did* and the *past form/infinitive* of the verb.

see Reference page 63

6　**a** Complete the questions from the interview with *did* or a question word. Then match the question to the answers. Check your answers in the tapescript on page 154.

1 _____ you get the money?

2 _____ did you go then?

3 _____ you have any money with you?

4 So _____ did you do?

a No, I didn't, not then.

b Yes, I did.

c I wanted to go to the Internet café ...

d I asked the old man for directions to the police station.

b Write questions for the sentences in Ex. 2b. Use these question words.

What time?　How many? Where?　Who?

What time did Robin disappear?

7　**a** What happened to Robin? Tell your partner your story and decide which ending you like best.

Student A: look at page 126.
Student B: look at page 129.

b 〔6.8〕 Listen. Which story is correct?

Person to person

8　Ask and answer. Find out what your partner did ...

yesterday　last night
last weekend
on their last holiday

You can ask only ten *yes/no* questions.

A: *Did you watch TV last night?*

B: *No, I didn't.*

Listening

9　**a** 〔6.9〕 Listen. Follow the directions on the map. Write the letters of these places.

post office ___　bookshop ___　police station ___

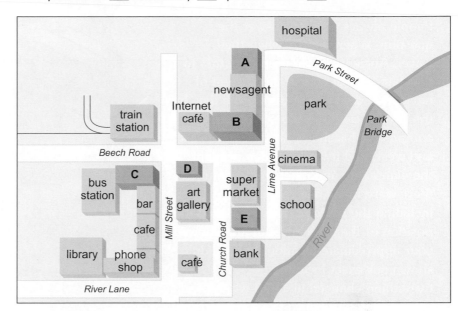

b Listen again and complete the expressions in the How to box. (You can check in the tapescript on page 155.)

HOW TO ...

ask for and give directions

Ask for directions	*Can you tell me the way to the bank?*
	(Excuse me,) do you know the way to _____?
Give directions	*Turn left at the _____.*
	Turn _____ Beech Road.
	Go straight on for about _____.
	Go along _____. It's on the left/right.
	It's at the end of _____.

10　Work in pairs. Use the map. Ask for and give directions.

from	to
the bank	the bridge
the police station	the bus station
the library	the cinema
the hospital	the art gallery

11　Write two or three sentences to answer your friend's question.

Can you email me directions from the station or bus stop to your house? Thanks, and see you on Saturday.

Grammar	Past Simple: negative
Can do	describe your last holiday

People always need to answer the question 'Where am I?' when they travel. Ancient people used the *stars* to navigate. But of course this system of navigation didn't work during the day. In the twelfth century sailors invented the *compass* – this shows north, south, east and west, and it works at day or night. In the eighteenth and nineteenth centuries there were many new inventions, including the *sextant*. This measured the position of the stars and sun and showed your approximate location, but it didn't show your exact location.

Everything changed in 1973 when the United States launched the 24 *satellites* of the Global Positioning System (GPS). These go around the Earth at a height of 17,440 kilometres. Computers combine the signals from the GPS satellites with *maps* to show exactly where you are and how to get to another place.

Reading

1 Discuss.

1 What do maps show?
2 Are you good at using them?
3 When was the last time you used a map?

2 a Read the text quickly. Choose the best title.

a What is GPS?
b How ancient people travelled
c Navigation past and present

b Read the text again. Use the words in italics to label the pictures below.

A _____

B _____

C _____

D _____

E _____

3 a Find words 1–6 in the text and match them to their meanings.

1 travel — a people who work on a ship
2 navigate — b not exact
3 sailors — c the place or position of something
4 approximate — d find your position or direction when you travel
5 location — e electronic communication between machines
6 signal — f go from one place to another

b Use information from the text to complete the sentences.

Ancient people *used* the stars to navigate.

1 The system of navigating by the stars _____ during the day.
2 There _____ many new inventions in the eighteenth century.
3 The sextant _____ an exact location.
4 In 1973 everything _____.

Grammar | Past Simple: negative

4 Read the sentence in the Active grammar box. Complete the rule. Choose the correct words.

> ### Active grammar
>
> *This system of navigation didn't work during the day.*
>
> To make negatives in the Past Simple we use *don't/didn't* and the *past form/infinitive* of the verb.

see Reference page 63

5 Correct these false statements.

Ancient people used compasses.

Ancient people didn't use compasses.

1 The sextant showed exact location.
2 People used cars in the sixteenth century.
3 Leonardo da Vinci invented the compass.
4 Ancient people played computer games.
5 Beethoven painted the *Mona Lisa*.
6 Marco Polo owned a mobile phone.

Vocabulary | transport

6 a Look at the photo and answer the questions.

1 How did people travel around Bangkok 100 years ago?
2 How do they get around today, do you think?

b Match the forms of transport to the famous places.

transport

1 red buses 2 yellow taxis 3 water buses
4 high speed trains 5 electric trams 6 bicycles

places

a Japan b London c San Francisco
d Amsterdam e Venice f New York

Person to person

7 Discuss.

1 How do you get around your town/city? (by car/bus, on foot, etc.)
2 Which form of transport do you like?

Pronunciation

8 a **6.10** Listen and <u>underline</u> the stressed words in the answers.

A: Do you like buses?
B: No, I like <u>trains</u>.

1 A: Did you visit Venice? B: No, we visited Rome.
2 A: Was it nice? B: No, it was horrible.

b Make dialogues using the table.

LIKE	VISIT	WAS IT
coffee? (✗ tea)	the cinema? (✗ the theatre)	small? (✗ big)
rice? (✗ pasta)	Russia? (✗ Poland)	new? (✗ old)
bikes? (✗ cars)	your uncle? (✗ my brother)	good? (✗ bad)

A: *Do you like coffee?* B: *No, I like tea.*

Writing

9 a Read the paragraph. <u>Underline</u> all the verbs in the Past Simple.

I visited Bangkok last year with my friend, Amanda. We liked the food but we didn't like the weather – it was very hot! We stayed in a hotel near the river. There were lots of tourists there and we talked to some girls from Australia. The city is enormous so we didn't walk very much. We travelled on the new overhead railway. It was very fast and comfortable. We looked at lots of temples and we watched the boats on the river. We wanted some presents so we visited the fantastic street markets ...

b Write a paragraph about your last holiday. Use the underlined verbs from Ex. 9a.

In shops

1 Discuss.

1 What can you see in the photo?

2 Do you use department stores? Which ones?

3 Why are department stores useful?

4 How do people move from one floor to another?

2 **a** **6.11** Listen to customers asking for information in a department store and complete the store guide.

STORE GUIDE	
Fourth floor	_____ • bedlinen • pharmacy
Third floor	children's clothes • _____ • restaurant
Second floor	women's clothes • women's shoes • hats
First floor	men's clothes • _____ • sports hall
Ground floor	beauty products • gifts • flowers • stationery
Basement	bookshop • _____ • electronic goods

b Listen again (or look at the tapescript on page 155) and complete the How to box.

<table>
<tr><td rowspan="5">HOW TO ...</td><td colspan="2">ask for what you want in a shop</td></tr>
<tr><td>Ask where something is</td><td>Where _____ men's shoes?</td></tr>
<tr><td>Ask for something</td><td>_____ a store guide?
Can _____ a copy, please?</td></tr>
<tr><td>Ask about prices</td><td>How _____ is that?</td></tr>
</table>

c In pairs, ask and answer about where to find things. Use the information in the store guide.

> ~~sofa~~ football CD player aspirin printer
> women's jeans pencil dictionary

A: *Where can I find a sofa?*

B: *In furniture on the fourth floor.*

3 Work in pairs. You can be an A pair or a B pair.

A pairs: you work in a gift shop. Turn to page 126.

B pairs: you are customers. Read the information below.

It is your best friend's birthday next week and you want to buy her two presents. Decide how much you want to spend, then look at the categories below and decide on two suitable presents.

• travel guide books

• DVDs

• chocolates

• gifts (wallets, diaries, address books)

• stationery (pens, pencils, notebooks)

Let's buy her a guide book to New York and a box of Swiss chocolates.

Write down the things you want to buy then talk to different A pairs and find the things you want.

Excuse me, have you got any Swiss chocolates?

How much are they?

Can I have a box?

Past Simple

Use the Past Simple to talk about actions and situations in the past. The actions and situations are finished.

*My hair **was** red when I was a girl, but it's grey now.*

to be

➕	I/He/She/It was	We/You/They were
➖	I/He/She/It wasn't (was not)	We/You/They weren't (were not)
❓	Was I/he/she/it?	Were we/you/they?
	Yes, I/he/she/it was.	Yes, we/you/they were.
	No, I/he/she/it wasn't.	No, we/you/they weren't.

*She **was** tired last night.*
*They **weren't** at the cinema yesterday.*
***Was** Karin at the office on Monday? No, she **wasn't**.*
***Were** the musicians good? Yes, they **were**.*

Regular verbs: positive

Make the Past Simple of most regular verbs by adding *-ed* to the verb.

*work → work**ed**, watch → watch**ed**, listen → listen**ed***

Note the spelling rules:

- add *-d* to verbs that end in *-e*,
  *live → liv**ed**, change → chang**ed***

- with verbs that end in consonant + *-y*, remove *-y* and add *-ied*, *study → stud**ied**, carry → carr**ied**.* (If the verb ends in vowel + *-y*, add *-ed*, *stay → stay**ed**.*)

- with verbs of one syllable that end in vowel + consonant, repeat the consonant and add *-ed*, *plan → plan**ned**, jog → jog**ged***

Negative

Did + not + infinitive

*Ancient people **did not use** compasses.*

In informal English, we use the contracted form *didn't*.

*People **didn't** know their exact location.*

Questions

Wh- questions

Wh-word + *did* + subject pronoun + infinitive
*When **did** you **finish** work yesterday?*

Yes/no questions

Did + subject pronoun + infinitive

Short answers

Yes, I/he/she/it/we/you/they did.
No, I/he/she/it/we/you/they didn't.
***Did** you **study** at university? Yes, I **did**.*

Prepositions of place

We use prepositions to show relationships of place. The prepositions *in, on, under, in front of, behind, between* and *next to* show clear location.

The books are **in** the cupboard. The picture is **on** the cupboard. The bin is **under** the desk. The chair is **in front of** the desk. The map is **behind** the desk. The desk is **next to** the cupboard. The plant is **between** the cupboard and the desk.

The preposition *at* can mean *in* or *near*.
I'm at the phone shop. (= in/in front of)
I'm at the door. (= next to/in front of)
We also use *at* with a very general meaning.
I'm at home. Are you at work?

Key vocabulary

Places in a town

art gallery   department store   pharmacy
bank   factory   phone shop   bar   police station
bookshop   hospital   post office   bridge
Internet café   restaurant   bus station   library
school   café   museum   square   cashpoint
newsagent's   supermarket   church   office
train station   tram   cinema   park

Forms of transport

bicycle   boat   bus   car   motorbike   ship   taxi
train   tram   water bus

1 Write the Past Simple form of the verbs in the correct column.

> ~~carry~~ ~~change~~ close decide ~~finish~~ ~~jog~~
> look live marry move own plan start
> stop want worry

+ -ed	+ -d	– -y + -ied	+ consonant + -ed
finished	changed	carried	jogged

2 There are ten mistakes in the text. Find and correct the other nine.

This is a photo of my great-grandparents – my mother's grandparents. They ~~live~~ *lived* in the middle of the last century. They was lovely people. My great-grandfather works in a car factory and he ownd a car when most people didn't know about them. My great-grandmother was very beautiful when she were a girl. She marryed my great-grandfather when she was only 17. She didn't work – she stays at home and looked after the children. My great-grandfather stoped work when he was 65, then every day they walked to the park and my great-grandmother always carries a little bag with sandwiches for their lunch. She died in 1983, when she was only 73, and after three months my great-grandfather dieed too – he didn't want to live without her.

3 Make Past Simple questions and answers from the prompts.

Albert Einstein/understand/Mathematics? (✓)

Q: Did Albert Einstein understand Mathematics?
A: Yes, he did.

Charles Darwin/French? (✗ British)
Q: Was Charles Darwin French?
A: No, he wasn' t. He was British.

1 Pablo Picasso/Spanish? (✓)
  Q: _____
  A: _____

2 Mozart /play/the guitar? (✗ the piano)
  Q: _____
  A: _____

3 President Kennedy/Russian? (✗ American)
  Q: _____
  A: _____

4 the USA/launch/GPS satellites in 1983? (✗ 1973)
  Q: _____
  A: _____

5 the Hoover Building/a factory/70 years ago? (✓)
  Q: _____
  A: _____

6 Alexander Graham Bell/invent/the computer? (✗ the telephone)
  Q: _____
  A: _____

7 the ancient Romans/speak Latin? (✓)
  Q: _____
  A: _____

8 Neil Armstrong/walk/on a star? (✗ the Moon)
  Q: _____
  A: _____

4 Complete the text with prepositions of place.

Alan's room is really untidy! He's got an armchair in the room but there are some shoes _on_ it and there's a plant (1)_____ it. There's a phone and some credit cards (2)_____ the bed and there are CDs and books (3)_____ it. There's a cup of cold coffee (4)_____ the bed! There's a newspaper (5)_____ the sink. His suitcase is on the floor, open, (6)_____ the desk and the sink, and his laptop is (7)_____ the suitcase.

5 Write the names of two places where you can do these things.

1 have something to eat or drink _____
2 buy things to take home _____
3 look at paintings or old things _____
4 start a journey _____
5 sit for a few minutes _____
6 ask people for help _____

7 People

Lead-in

1 **a** Complete the descriptions of the people in the photos with A-H.

1 _C_ has got a pretty face.
2 _____ has got blue eyes.
3 _____ has got fair hair.
4 _____ has got dark skin.
5 _____ has got grey hair.

6 _____ has got a beard.
7 _____ is slim.
8 _____ is young.
9 _____ is bald.
10 _____ wears glasses.

b **7.1** Listen and compare your answers.

2 Work in pairs.

Student A: describe a person from the photos.

This person's got fair hair and wears glasses.

Student B: point at the person.

3 **a** Who does it belong to? Match the things 1–4 with the people/ places a–d.

1 Buckingham Palace
2 *The Mona Lisa*
3 20th Century Fox
4 Microsoft

a Rupert Murdoch
b Bill Gates
c Queen Elizabeth II
d The Louvre

b Check your answers in pairs.

A: *Who does Buckingham Palace belong to?*

B: *It belongs to Queen Elizabeth II.*

Reading and vocabulary

1 Marianne is twenty-two. She comes from New Zealand, but is at university in Brazil. Discuss.

1 Where is the beach in the photo?

2 What is the connection between Marianne and the beach, do you think?

Dear Carol

A Thanks for your letter about my old friends in New Zealand!

B Everything is fine here. I arrived in Rio de Janeiro a month ago to start my course and then I moved in with my host family. They live in a big apartment near the beach in Ipanema.

C The family is very nice. Mr and Mrs Silva are middle-aged and very friendly. They've got three children. Tina is my age, she's got dark hair and she's pretty. She's tall, like me. João is the middle one; he's fifteen. He's quite short and he's very tanned from playing football! Carlos is the young one, he's a bit fat. He's lovely, he laughs all the time.

D Every morning I go to college. The classes are tiring, especially the literature ones. I usually go to the beach in the afternoon. The beach here is beautiful and the sea is warm. There is a really handsome man on the beach. He watches me every day. I think he's nice but I'm quite shy so I don't look at him!

E Write to me soon and tell me all your news.

Love

Marianne

2 **a** Read the letter and answer the questions.

1 What did Marianne do a month ago?

2 Who does she live with now?

3 What does she do in the afternoon?

b Read the letter again. Match the people and the adjectives.

1	Mr and Mrs Silva	a	tanned, short
2	Tina	b	handsome, nice
3	João	c	friendly, middle-aged
4	Carlos	d	dark, pretty
5	the man on the beach	e	tall, shy
6	Marianne	f	young, fat

Lifelong learning

Opposite adjectives

A good way to remember adjectives is in pairs with opposite meanings.

old – young

3 **a** Find adjectives in Ex. 2b with the opposite meaning.

pale *tanned*

1 fair _____ 2 slim _____ 3 horrible _____
4 ugly _____/_____ 5 old _____ 6 tall _____

b Put the adjectives from Ex. 3a in the correct column. Which adjectives can go in more than one column?

BODY	FACE	SKIN	HAIR	HEIGHT	AGE	PERSONALITY
		tanned				

4 Think of someone in your class, or a famous person. Describe him/her to your partner but don't say his/her name! Can your partner guess the person?

She's quite short. She's got dark hair ...

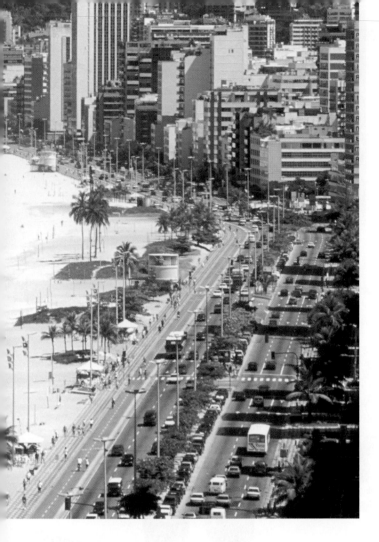

Grammar | pronoun *one/ones*

5 a Read the sentences in the Active grammar box and choose the correct meaning for the <u>underlined</u> words.

> ### Active grammar
>
> 1 *They've got three children. João is the middle <u>one</u>.*
> 2 *The classes are tiring, especially the literature <u>ones</u>.*
>
> **Meanings**
>
> a) classes b) class c) student d) child

see Reference page 73

b Read the paragraph. Find four more words you can change to *one* (or *ones*).

When I was a child I lived in three different houses. The first ~~house~~ *one* was lovely. The second house was quite small, but it was in a nice location. The third house wasn't very nice but there were six bedrooms. I used the bedroom on the second floor. The other bedrooms were on the first floor.

Listening

6 a [7.2] Listen to the song and answer these questions.

1 Is the singer happy or sad? Why?
2 Who is 'The Girl from Ipanema', do you think?

b Listen again and complete the gaps.

> Tall and (1) _____ and (2) _____ and lovely
> The girl from Ipanema (3) _____ walking
> And when she passes, each (4) _____ she passes goes – ah
> When she (5) _____, she's like a samba
> That swings so cool (6) _____ sways so gentle
> That when she passes, each (7) _____ she passes goes – ooh
>
> (Ooh) But I (8) _____ her so sadly
> How can I tell (9) _____ I love her
> Yes, I would (10) _____ my heart gladly
> But each day, when she walks to the (11) _____
> She looks straight ahead, (12) _____ at me
>
> Tall and (13) _____ and (14) _____ and lovely
> The girl from (15) _____ goes walking
> And when she pauses, I smile – but she doesn't see (doesn't see)
> She (16) _____ see, she never sees me ...

Writing

7 a Match the statements to paragraphs A–E in Marianne's letter in Ex. 2.

Marianne describes her host family.	C
She asks Carol to do something.	☐
She thanks Carol.	☐
What she does.	☐
Where she lives.	☐

b Complete the How to box with words and phrases from Marianne's letter.

> **HOW TO ...**
>
> ### start and finish informal letters
>
> | Start | (all letters) _____ + first name |
> |---|---|
> | Finish | (close friends/family) _____ + your name |
> | | (friends) *Best wishes* + your name |

8 Your family is a 'host family' for foreign students. Sue, an English friend, wants to stay with you. Write a letter to Sue and tell her about where you live and your family.

Listening

1 a Jane Birch has a lot of friends. Match their names to the photos.

Mrs Clark wears glasses.	☐
Davy has got brown hair.	☐
Tara is quite tall.	☐
Mr Clark's got a grey beard.	☐
Gordon is bald.	☐

b Add information to the descriptions in Ex. 1a. Then make guesses about each person's job.

Mrs Clark's got grey hair. I think she's retired.

2 a Jane has got some presents for her friends. Match the words to the things in the picture.

clock ☐	electric drill ☐	wrapping paper ☐
diary ☐	trainers $\boxed{A}$	handbag ☐	umbrella ☐

b Who are the presents for? Discuss. Give reasons for your answers.

I think the handbag is for Tara because ...

c 7.3 Jane went to work this morning. Her husband, Mike, phoned and asked her about the presents. Listen and check your answers to Ex. 2b.

Grammar | possessive pronouns

3 **a** Look at these examples. Choose the correct meaning (a–d) for the underlined words.

a our umbrella   b belong to Davy

c Davy's trainers   d belongs to us

1 A: The trainers. Are they Davy's?
   B: Yes, the trainers are his.

2 A: There's an umbrella on the table.
   B: It's ours!

b Read the tapescript on page 155 and complete the Active grammar box.

Active grammar

Possessive adjectives	Possessive pronouns
my	____
his	____
her	____
its	*its*
our	____
your	____
their	____

see Reference page 73

4 Rewrite the sentences. Use a possessive pronoun (and a verb if necessary) to replace the phrases in italics.

These aren't my CDs, they *belong to Jane*.

These aren't my CDs, they're hers.

1 Excuse me. Is this *your bag*?
2 Use the blue pen; the red one *belongs to me*.
3 Is this *Maria's watch*?
4 The house next to the church *belonged to them*.
5 Are these sandwiches *for us*?
6 That wasn't her phone number, it was *John's*.
7 They weren't our dogs, they were *Bob and Jo's*.
8 *Does* this *belong to your brother*?

Pronunciation

5 **a** **7.4** Listen to the *th* sound /θ/ in the word *birthday*. Is it the same as the sound in *bro**th**er* or *ba**th**room*?

b **7.5** Listen and circle the words you hear.

1 a) sick b) thick   4 a) first b) thirst
2 a) sink b) think   5 a) tree b) three
3 a) free b) three

c **7.6** Listen. Do you hear the sound /θ/? Tick (✓) for yes, cross (✗) for no. Listen and repeat.

1 ☐ 2 ☐ 3 ☐ 4 ☐ 5 ☐ 6 ☐ 7 ☐ 8 ☐

Vocabulary | ordinal numbers/months

6 **a** When are Jane's friends' birthdays? Look at the tapescript on page 155.

Gordon *the third of next month* Davy _____
Tara _____

b Write the numbers from Ex. 6a on the red lines then complete the table.

1 _____	6 _____	11 _____	20 _____
2 *second*	7 _____	12 _____	22 *twenty-second*
3 _____	8 *eighth*	13 _____	30 _____
4 *fourth*	9 _____	14 *fourteenth*	31 _____
5 _____	10 _____	15 _____	

c **7.7** Listen and check your answers. Then repeat.

7 Choose the correct words.

1 My birthday is on the *first/one* of May.
2 Our new house has got *three/third* bedrooms.
3 America's Independence Day is on the *four/fourth* of July.
4 This is my *three/third* holiday this year!
5 It's Lucy's *nine/ninth* birthday on Saturday.

8 **a** Find the names of two months in Ex. 7.

b Number the months 1–12 in the correct order.

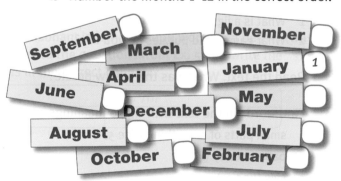

c In pairs, answer the questions.

When is your birthday?

What dates are holidays in your country?

9 **a** Talk to your classmates. Find a student/students with:

1 a birthday in the same month as yours.
2 the first and last birthdays of the year.
3 a birthday this month.
4 a birthday next month.
5 a birthday last month.

b Write the names of all the students in your class, in order of their birthdays.

1 Read the dialogue. Find seven words you can change to *one* or *ones*.

A: There are so many sofas here, Philip. Which ~~sofas~~ do you like?   *ones*

B: Well, I like the brown ~~sofa~~.   *one*

A: No, it's ugly. What about the red sofa?

B: It's OK.

A: Fine. Now, chairs. Do you like modern chairs?

B: Yes. I like those chairs in the corner.

A: The metal chairs?

B: Yes.

A: Yes, they're quite nice. But how about this chair?

B: No, I don't like that chair. It isn't very attractive.

A: Well, I don't like this shop. Let's go to a different shop.

2 Match questions 1–7 with the questions with the same meaning.

1 Does this bag belong to you?
2 Is this his?
3 Is this Mary's CD player?
4 Are these our letters?
5 Are these theirs?
6 Is this present for me?
7 Are these mine or yours?
8 Does this umbrella belong to us?

a Are these ours?
b Is this hers?
c Is this mine?
d Do these books belong to them?
e Is this yours?
f Is this ours?
g Are these my keys or your keys?
h Does this belong to Mr McBride?

3 Complete these texts with the correct Past Simple form of the verbs in brackets.

Madame Chiang Kai-Shek died on Thursday in New York. She was 106. Madame Chiang Kai-Shek *met* (meet) her famous husband – Taiwan's leader Chiang Kai Shek – in 1920 and she married him in 1927. After her husband died in 1975 she (1) _____ (leave) Taiwan, and because she (2) _____ (speak) English, she (3) _____ (come) to the United States and (4) _____ (spend) most of her time in Manhattan.

4 Complete the sentences with ordinal numbers. The numbers in the box are clues.

| 1 | 8 | 9 | 16 | 18 | 25 |

Abraham Lincoln was the *sixteenth* president of the United States.

1 August is the _____ month of the year.
2 Christmas Day is on the _____ of December.
3 Neil Armstrong was the _____ man on the Moon.
4 British people can vote after their _____ birthday.
5 The _____ series of *Friends* was the last one.

5 Match the verbs and prepositions, then complete the sentences. (You need the Past Simple in one sentence.)

1 hand   a together
2 give   b up
3 look   c in
4 put   d back
5 pick   e at

Please *hand in* your completed forms to the tour guide.

1 Oh no! This dish is in pieces! Can you _____ it _____ again?
2 _____ your rubbish _____, please. Don't leave it on the floor.
3 Can you _____ _____ the dictionary when you finish your work?
4 A: How do you know the answer?
   B: I _____ _____ my grammar book.

Robert Atkins, famous for the Atkins Diet, died yesterday aged 72 after a fall in the street. Atkins, a doctor, studied at the University of Michigan. He (5) _____ (become) quite fat after he left university and he tried different diets to lose weight. He (6) _____ (think) that people (7) _____ (have) problems with weight because they (8) _____ (eat) the wrong things, and he (9) _____ (write) his first diet book in 1970. Not many people (10) _____ (buy) the book at first, but Atkins's diet is now very popular and his books are bestsellers.

A

B

8 Day to day

C

D

E

Lead-in

1 Answer the questions about photos A and B.

1 Where are the people?

2 What are the seasons? (spring, summer, autumn, winter)

2 **a** Check the words in a dictionary. Then find them in the photos. Which photo are they in? Write A–E.

coat B   hat ☐   jacket ☐   jeans ☐   pullover ☐   scarf ☐   shorts ☐
skirt ☐   suit ☐   T-shirt ☐   trainers ☐

b Can you name any other clothes in the photos?

3 **a** Match the clothes adjectives (1–6) with their meanings (a–f).

1	formal	a	comfortable, not small
2	casual	b	not thick or heavy
3	tight	c	tidy, in good condition
4	light	d	for important events, for business
5	loose	e	comfortable and informal
6	smart	f	feel small, fit closely

b **8.1** Describe the clothes in photos C–E. Then listen and check.

C – a smart suit

c Do you agree with these statements? Why/Why not?

1 I think jeans are uncomfortable.

2 It's OK to wear shorts to formal business meetings.

3 Winter coats are usually light.

4 Tight shirts and pullovers look good.

1 Choose the best word or phrase.

I am quite fit because I *hardly ever/often* play sport.

1 Russians wear heavy coats in the winter because it is *never/usually* cold.

2 I don't like formal clothes. I *sometimes/hardly ever* wear a suit and tie!

3 Dario is quite fat because he *always/hardly ever* eats a lot.

4 Vegetarians *sometimes/never* eat meat.

5 Swiss watches *sometimes/hardly ever* cost a lot of money.

2 a Write the *-ing* form of these verbs.

come   *coming*

1	dig	_____	7	study	_____
2	make	_____	8	swim	_____
3	plan	_____	9	use	_____
4	read	_____	10	wait	_____
5	ride	_____	11	write	_____
6	sit	_____	12	carry	_____

b Sandra is writing a letter to her friend. Complete the gaps with some of the verbs from Ex. 2a in the Present Continuous.

Dear Geena
Thanks for your letter. I *'m sitting* in Luigi's café at the moment – do you remember it? We had a really good meal here in March. I (1) _____ this letter from here because I (2) _____ for Jacob. He's at college at the moment; he (3) _____ Art. He (4) _____ a computer in his Art classes and he really enjoys it – he (5) _____ some amazing pictures on the computer. There's a travel guide to Canada on the table – do you know why? I (6) _____ it because Jacob and I (7) _____ a visit to Canada! Really! We want to ...

3 Write questions and answers.

sun shine ✗ (rain)

Is the sun shining? No, the sun isn't shining. It's raining.

1 you/read/good book ✓

2 you/study German ✗ (English)

3 she/cook dinner ✗ (prepare tomorrow's lunch)

4 he/work at home today ✓

5 they/play tennis ✗ (badminton)

4 Read the paragraph. Then write sentences in the Present Simple or the Present Continuous.

Amélie is a computer programmer. She works in a big, formal office. She has one hour for lunch. Today is her office summer excursion – every year they take their clients out for the day and buy them a big lunch. Today they are at a football match.

use/computer
Amélie usually uses a computer.

take/photos/match
She's taking photos of the football match today.

1 wear/formal business suit

2 wear/jeans and a T-shirt

3 talk/to people in the office

4 talk/to clients at the match

5 have/sandwich for lunch in the office

6 have/big meal in a restaurant

5 a Match the adverbs with their opposites.

1 badly   a fast
2 happily   b carefully
3 slowly   c quietly
4 loudly   d uncomfortably
5 carelessly   e well
6 comfortably   f unhappily

b Complete the sentences with an adverb from Ex. 5a.

1 Julie watched Philip *unhappily*.

2 He's shouting _____.

3 They're sitting _____.

4 'Shh! Please talk _____!'

5 She's writing her essay very _____.

6 Complete the sentences with suitable clothes.

I wear *shorts and a T-shirt* when it's sunny.

1 I wear _____ when it's snowing.

2 I wear _____ when it's raining.

3 I wear _____ for a country walk.

4 I wear _____ when I go to parties.

5 I wear _____ when I go to work.

6 I wear _____ for formal meetings.

9 | Culture

Lead-in

1 **a** Put the letters in the correct order and match the art forms to the photos.

1 S C I U M _____ ☐
2 M I L F _____ ☐
3 R E T H E A T _____ ☐
4 A N I G N I P T _____ ☐

b Look at the words and phrases in the box. In pairs, name one example of each.

> ballet cartoon classical music comedy dance horror literature
> modern art novels opera plays painting poetry rock music sculpture

2 **a** Complete the word map with the art forms from Ex. 1a and words and phrases from the box. Then compare with a partner.

b 9.1 Listen to two people. Is your word map the same as theirs?

c Add more words to your word map if you can.

3 Work in groups. Discuss the questions. What or who is your favourite:
- film? • book? • play? • opera or ballet? • classical composer?
- poem? • painting? • group or singer?

Reading

1 **a** Discuss.

1   What's in the news today?

2   How did you get the news stories?

3   How do you usually get the news?

b Label the photos (1–6) with the names of the news sources from Ex. 2a.

Vocabulary | news media

2 **a** Look at the text and tick (✓) the correct adjectives in the table.

	fast	easy	detailed	cheap	new	exciting	versatile
Newspapers							
The radio							
The TV							
Teletext							
The Internet							
Text messages							

b Read the text carefully. Find advantages (good things) and disadvantages (bad things) about the different news sources. Can you think of any other advantages and disadvantages?

Advantages: *Newspapers are cheap and versatile. The radio is relaxing.*

Disadvantages: *The radio is old-fashioned.*

c Do you agree with the opinions in the text?

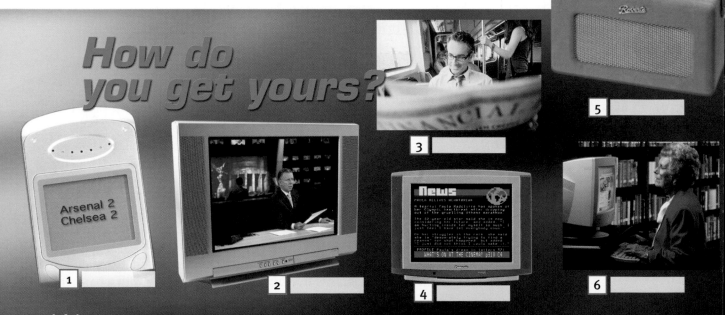

How do you get yours?

Arsenal 2
Chelsea 2

1 **2** **3** **4** **5** **6**

News

We all like to know what's in the news – world news, local news, sports news – and today there are many different ways of finding out about recent events. How do people choose, and what do they like about the different methods?

Newspapers – still the old favourite. Millions of people read newspapers because they're cheap, detailed and also versatile – you can read them at home, at work or on the train.

The radio – people listen to the radio because it's easy. You can listen in the car, when you're working or in bed, but some people think the radio is old-fashioned.

The TV – almost everyone watches TV and a lot of people get the news from it. It's interesting and exciting, because it's visual. There are lots of different news programmes to suit all types of people.

Teletext – this is a fast way of getting the news, but it doesn't give you a lot of detail.

The Internet – many people now use the Internet. It's detailed and it's very fast: news stories appear when they happen; but it can be expensive.

Text messaging – this way of getting news is popular because it's fast and very new. Messages arrive on your mobile phone, so you get the news immediately, but it is expensive.

Grammar | comparison of adjectives

3 **a** **9.2** Listen and complete the sentences with the correct news sources.

1 _____ are <u>cheaper than</u> the Internet.
2 _____ is <u>faster than</u> TV.
3 _____ is <u>more detailed than</u> teletext.
4 _____ is <u>more exciting than</u> newspapers.
5 _____ is <u>easier than</u> newspapers.
6 _____ is <u>better than</u> the radio.

b Complete the Active grammar box with the <u>underlined</u> words in Ex. 3a.

Active grammar

Adjective	Comparative
fast	*faster than*
cheap	_____
easy	_____
detailed	_____
exciting	_____
good	_____
bad	*worse than*

Write suitable comparative adjectives next to the rules.

1 Add -er to adjectives with one syllable only: *faster*
2 With adjectives that end in -y, remove the -y and add -ier: _____
3 With longer adjectives, we use *more* before the adjective: _____
4 Some adjectives have irregular comparatives: _____

see Reference page 93

4 Complete the sentences with the comparative form of the adjectives and another news source. Then compare with a partner.

TV news is ... (exciting)

more exciting than newspapers.

1 Teletext is ... (immediate)
2 Newspapers are ... (detailed)
3 Text messaging is ... (modern)
4 The radio is ... (good)

5 Write comparative sentences about the pictures.

1 Newspapers are usually more serious than magazines.

Pronunciation

6 **a** **9.3** Listen to these phrases and <u>underline</u> the syllables with /ə/. Listen again and repeat.

eas<u>ier</u> th<u>an</u>

1 faster than
2 colder than
3 healthier than

b Write sentences comparing these things. Then read your sentences to a partner.

1 Iceland/Egypt/cold
2 Spanish/English/easy
3 fruit/chocolate/healthy
4 a Ferrari/a Fiat/fast

Writing and speaking

7 **a** Complete the table.

	I like ...	I don't like ...
TV programmes	*The Simpsons*	*Friends*
newspapers		
film stars		
books		
types of food		
holidays		

b Write sentences comparing the things in the table. Give reasons.

I like 'The Simpsons' because it's funnier than 'Friends'.

c Compare your sentences with a partner.

8 In groups, compare what you like.

A: *I like 'The Simpsons'.*
B: *I don't. I like 'The Sopranos' because it's more exciting than 'The Simpsons'.*

1 Put the words in the correct order to make sentences.

been to China Have ever you ?

Have you ever been to China?

1 never a long-haul I've flight been on

2 adventure holiday you been Have ever on an ?

3 to We've New York and Boston been

4 horse-riding in been She's Scotland

2 Some of the past participles in these sentences are wrong. Tick (✓) the correct sentences. Cross (✗) the incorrect ones and write the correct past participle.

Have you visited the wax museum? ☑ _____

Jonathan has ~~saw~~ a very good film. ☒ *seen*

1 I've spended a lot of money. ☐ _____

2 We've never bought a new car. ☐ _____

3 Has she took her last exam yet? ☐ _____

4 We've never play volleyball. ☐ _____

5 Mum and Dad haven't arrived yet. ☐ _____

6 He has wrote over 100 books. ☐ _____

3 Max and Lorena are on holiday in India. Look at the list of things they have/haven't done and complete Max's postcard.

	Max	Lorena
see the Taj Mahal	✓	✓
visit the Bollywood studios	✗	✗
have lots of Indian meals	✗	✓
go swimming in the Indian Ocean	✓	✗
take an elephant ride	✓	✓
buy some spices	✗	✓
play golf with some friends	✓	✗
go on a boat trip	✓	✓

Dear Paul

Well, we're in India – the holiday of a lifetime! *We've seen* the Taj Mahal – it's amazing – but *we haven't visited* the Bollywood studios. (1) _____ lots of Indian meals, of course – she loves Indian food – but I have only eaten in the hotel. (2) _____ in the Indian Ocean. Lorena hasn't because she's worried about sharks! (3) _____ an elephant ride. That was interesting but not very comfortable. (4) _____ some spices from the market and (5) _____ with some friends. (6) _____ on a boat trip. It was really relaxing.

See you soon.

Love Max

4 Find the mistakes in the Past Simple/Present Perfect in this dialogue, and correct them.

Liz: Have you ever been skiing?

Sue: No, I ~~didn't~~. *haven't*

Liz: It's fantastic.

Sue: When did you go?

Liz: We've been last winter.

Sue: And where did you go?

Liz: Switzerland.

Sue: I never went to Switzerland. Was it nice?

Liz: Yes, it was beautiful.

Sue: Was it cold?

Liz: Yes, we've been in January so it was very cold.

Sue: Did you ever go there in the summer?

Liz: No, I haven't.

5 Complete the sentences with a verb in the box.

swim take go commute fly pay drive

Flying in business class is quite expensive.

1 _____ by credit card is very convenient.

2 _____ is a good way to get fit.

3 _____ to the cinema is my favourite activity.

4 _____ a fast car is very exciting.

5 _____ photos is the best part of a holiday.

6 _____ takes a long time in big cities.

6 Complete each sentence with a travel word.

1 It doesn't stop. It's a _____ flight.

2 Excuse me. Can I have a _____ ticket? I want to come back tomorrow.

3 I prefer flying in business _____ because the seats are more comfortable.

4 Trains to Edinburgh leave from _____ 10.

5 I park my car on the street because I don't have a _____.

6 A Boeing 747 can take more than 300 _____.

7 Write the type of holiday where you can do these activities.

1 swimming and surfing _____

2 swimming and sunbathing _____

3 visiting museums and art galleries _____

4 skiing _____

5 walking and cycling _____

11 Learning

Lead-in

1   Look at the photos. What are the four learning situations? Which ones have you been in?

2   **a** Which learning situation does each rule come from?

   1   Drive on the left.
   2   Speak English.
   3   Follow my movements.
   4   Don't go over the speed limit.
   5   Put your right hand here.
   6   Don't shout out the answers.

   b Discuss.

   1   What were the main rules when you were at school?
   2   Did you usually obey them?
   3   What was the punishment when you broke the rules?

3   **a** Put the words and phrases in the box into two groups: school subjects or educational institutions.

   > Biology   Chemistry   college   Geography   History   kindergarten
   > Languages   Mathematics   Physics   polytechnic   primary school
   > Science   secondary school   university

   b **11.1** Listen and write the number of syllables for each word in the box. Which word has the most syllables? Listen again and check your answers.

   Bi/o/lo/gy – four

   c How many other school subjects can you add to the list?

No more continents?

For centuries natural barriers such as rivers, mountains and seas have made travel difficult. Now, with modern technology, we are crossing these barriers and the world is becoming a much smaller place. Britain was an island for 8,000 years. But the Channel Tunnel opened in 1994 and connected Britain to mainland Europe. The Oresund Bridge and Tunnel opened in 2000 and connected Sweden to Denmark and the rest of Europe. Now there are more projects to link different parts of the world. The Italian government is going to build a 5km-long bridge between Sicily and the Italian mainland, and in Asia, Indonesia is going to build a tunnel between the islands of Java and Sumatra.

But there are bigger projects, to join continents! Spain and Morocco are going to build a tunnel connecting Europe to Africa. They are thinking of building a 38km tunnel between Punta Palomas on the south coast of Spain and Punta Malabata in northern Morocco, near Tangier. And the United States and Russia are discussing a project to connect Alaska to Siberia, joining the continents of North America and Asia.

Reading and vocabulary

1 Look at the map. Answer the questions.

1 How many continents are there? What are they?

2 How do we travel between continents?

2 **a** Read the text quickly. Is it about:

1 the past and the present?

2 the past, the present and the future?

3 the present and the future?

b Read the text again and match the places. Then match the pairs to A–F on the map.

1	Java	a	the Italian mainland		☐
2	Sicily	b	Denmark		☐
3	Britain	c	Sumatra		*E*
4	Alaska	d	mainland Europe		☐
5	Sweden	e	Morocco		☐
6	Spain	f	Siberia		☐

3 **a** Look at the words in the box and <u>underline</u> them in the text. Then find:

1 three verbs with the same meaning.

2 three words connected with geography.

3 three adjectives.

> continent difficult modern island connect
> mainland link different join

b Complete the questions about the text with words from the box in Ex. 3a, then write the answers.

1 Which natural barriers make travel _____?

2 When did a tunnel _____ Britain to mainland Europe?

3 What is going to link Java with the _____ of Sumatra?

4 Which _____ is Siberia part of?

Grammar | *be going to*

4 Look at these sentences and tick (✓) the correct explanation.

In the years to come the world is going to be a much smaller place.
Spain and Morocco are going to build a tunnel.

We use *going to* for:

1 intentions (things people plan to do in the future) ☐
2 things happening now ☐

5 Complete the Active grammar box.

Active grammar

	I	We/You/They	He/She/It
➕	'm (am) going to + infinitive	____ going to + infinitive	____ going to + infinitive
➖	'm (am) not going to + infinitive	aren't (are not) going to + infinitive	isn't (____) going to + infinitive
❓	Am I going to + infinitive?	____ we, you, they going to + infinitive?	____ he, she, it going to + infinitive?

see Reference page 123

6 Write sentences and questions with *be going to* using the prompts.

Ford/build/a new electric car
Ford is going to build a new electric car.

your company/open/a new office/next year/?
Is your company going to open a new office next year?

1 Britain/not/build/any more airports
2 my parents/retire/next year
3 they/open/a new bridge/in 2020
4 the Americans/build/a space station/?
5 I/start/a new course/in September
6 we/not/have/a holiday/next summer

Pronunciation

7 **a** **12.2** Listen. What do you notice about the pronunciation of *to*?
I'm <u>going</u> to stop <u>smoking</u>

b **12.3** Listen and repeat these sentences, then mark the stress.
1 She's going to lose weight.
2 They're going to sell their car.
3 We're going to learn French.
4 I'm going to buy a laptop.

Vocabulary | future time

8 **a** Put the time expressions in the correct order.

next week ~~today~~
in two years' time
next summer ~~tomorrow~~
three years from now
later this year
the week after next

1 today 2 tomorrow

b In pairs, ask and answer about your intentions using the time expressions.

A: *What are you going to do tomorrow?*

Person to person

9 **a** Interview your partner about his/her intentions. Use the ideas below and some of the verbs in the box to make questions. Write down the answers.

1 health   4 holidays
2 work   5 friends/family
3 entertainment   6 sport

> do visit watch get
> start join meet change
> improve buy travel

A: *Are you going to improve your health?*

b Compare your information with other pairs.

Speaking

10 Work in groups of four.
Student A: turn to page 128.
Student B: turn to page 128.
Student C: turn to page 128.
Student D: Talk to the students in your group. Ask them questions and find someone who is going to:

1 change their job soon.
2 write a novel before they retire.
3 have more than three children.

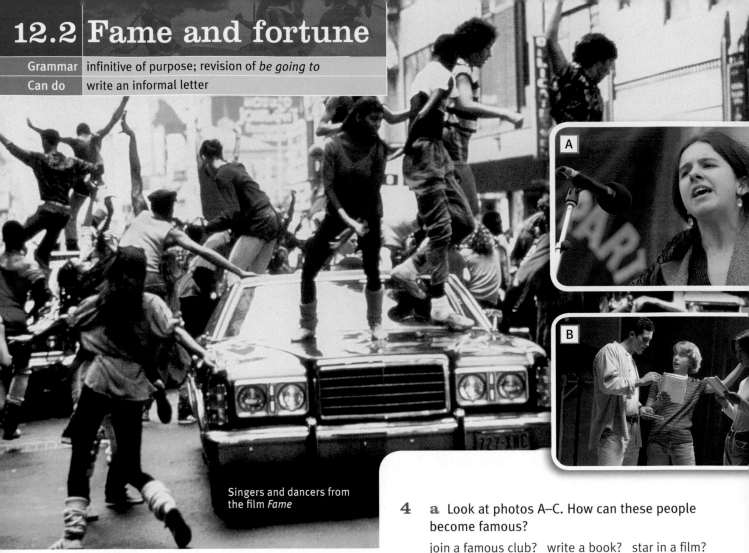

Singers and dancers from the film *Fame*

A

B

Listening

1 How can people become famous? Make a list.

enter a 'pop star' competition

be on a reality TV show

2 **a** **12.4** Listen to the song *Fame!* and tick (✓) the correct sentence.

1 The singer is famous. ☐

2 The singer wants to be famous in the future. ☐

b Look at the scene from the film *Fame!* and answer the questions.

1 What is it about?

2 How are these people going to become famous?

3 Listen again and put the lines of the chorus in the correct order.

I'm going to live forever	☐
I'm going to make it to heaven	☐
I feel it coming together	☐
People will see me and cry	☐
Fame!	1
Baby, remember my name!	☐
I'm going to learn how to fly	☐
Light up the sky like a flame	☐
I'm going to live forever	☐

4 **a** Look at photos A–C. How can these people become famous?

join a famous club? write a book? star in a film? become President? win a competition?

b Use a dictionary. Match three phrases from the box to photos A–C.

> politician training session acting drama election a play politics football team ball control skills

5 **a** **12.5** Listen to three interviews and match them to photos A–C.

b Listen again and choose the correct answer.

1 Victoria is a) a university student or b) a TV producer.

2 Helena is a) a politician or b) a student.

3 Lewis is in a) the first team or b) the reserve team.

c Listen again and write sentences with *be going to*. Then match your sentences with reasons a–c.

Victoria _____

Helena _____

Lewis _____

a to get a place in a professional team

b to become a famous performer

c to learn more about elections

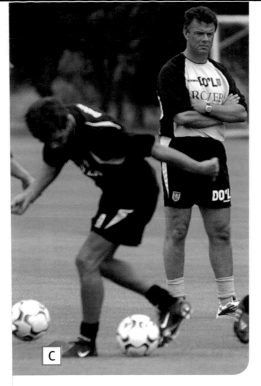

C

Grammar | infinitive
of purpose

6 Look at what Lewis said and choose the correct answer.

I'm going to practise with them twice a week to improve my physical fitness.

I'm going to work really hard to get into the first team.

What does the underlined phrase do?

a It explains the purpose or reason for something.

b It gives more information about the verb.

see Reference page 123

7 Read the sentences. Are the reasons true for you? If not, change them so they are true for you.

I go on holiday to sunbathe and get tanned.

No, I go on holiday to visit new places.

1 I learn English to get a better job.

2 I go to nightclubs to meet new people.

3 I watch television to find out about other countries.

4 I go to work to have fun and relax.

5 I listen to pop music to improve my mind.

Reading and writing

8 **a** Read this letter from Victoria (from Ex. 5) to Josie and tick (✓) the correct sentence.

1 Josie is Victoria's sister.

2 Josie is Victoria's best friend.

Dear Josie

Thank you very much for your last letter. It was great to hear about your holiday in Cornwall. But I was sorry to hear that the weather was so bad.
Everything is going well here. My course is interesting and I've met a lot of nice people. The other students are very friendly. The most exciting thing is the drama group. I joined it last month and I'm really enjoying it. We're going to do a play at the end of term and I'm going to have one of the main parts! A TV company is making a film about the university and they are going to film the show. Yes, your little sister is going to be famous!
Write soon and give my love to Mum and Dad.

Love,
Victoria

b Read the letter again and discuss these questions in pairs.

1 How do we know that Victoria has had a letter from Josie?

2 How do we know this is a letter between relatives or close friends?

3 Why does Victoria use exclamation marks (!)?

9 Complete the How to box with the underlined expressions in the letter.

HOW TO ...	**organise an informal letter**	
	Begin by mentioning the last letter you received	_____
	Make a positive comment about it	_____
	Describe your feelings	_____
	Say something general about your life	_____
	Make a request to end the letter	_____

10 Write a letter to a relative or close friend. Use Victoria's letter as a model. Follow these steps.

1 Make notes about your life now.

2 Make notes about your future plans.

3 Organise your notes into paragraphs.

4 Write the letter.

5 Check for grammar and spelling. Correct any mistakes.

6 Swap letters with a partner and check the spelling and grammar. Help your partner correct the mistakes.

A

B

C

1 Look at the photos and discuss the questions.

1 Can you match the photos with these cities: London, New York, Sydney, Paris, Bilbao?

2 Do you know these cities? What do you like/dislike about them?

3 Do you know any of the buildings in the photos?

4 Can you think of any other famous buildings in these cities?

2 Can you find an example of each of these words/phrases in the photos? Use your dictionary.

1 a skyscraper
2 an amazing shape
3 a roof

4 something made of stone
5 something made of glass
6 something made of metal

3 Look at some facts and figures about five buildings in these cities. Watch the film and tick (✓) the correct building in the table.

	The Flatiron Building	The Guggenheim Museum	The Eiffel Tower	The Gherkin	The Sydney Opera House
1 It opened in 1889.			✓		
2 It has 19 galleries.					
3 It opened over 30 years ago.					
4 It's made of stone and metal.					
5 It's only two metres wide.					
6 It opened in 2004.					
7 It's 300 metres high.					
8 Its roof comes from Sweden.					
9 It's 87 metres high.					
10 The architect was Danish.					

4 Discuss.

1 Which building from the film do you like most? Why?

2 Do you like old buildings or new buildings? Why?

3 Do you have a favourite building in your country? What is it, and why?

D

E

7 Great Expectations

1 Charles Dickens was a British writer from the 19th century. Do you know any of his books? Do you know the films in the photos?

2 Complete the sentences with words from the box. Use a dictionary.

> broken   scary   scared   come along   novel   wedding dress

1 *Great Expectations* is a _____ by Charles Dickens.
2 When women get married they wear a _____.
3 I am _____ of water because I can't swim.
4 *Alien* and *The Exorcist* are very _____ films.
5 I can't use my DVD player now because it's _____.
6 Don't stand there! _____, we're late!

3 Now watch the film extract from *Great Expectations* and match the adjectives with the people and places.

	the boy (Pip)	the girl (Estella)	the woman (Miss Havisham)	the house
dark				✓
large				
old				
pretty				
rich				
scared				
scary				
shy				
strange				
thin				
young				

4 Discuss.

1 Did you like the extract?
2 Do you like old films?
3 What is the relationship between Miss Havisham and Pip?
4 Why does the clock on the house show the wrong time?
5 What happens next, do you think?

1 Do you know any famous carnivals? When and where do they happen?

2 In pairs, describe the photos. Answer the questions.
   1 What are the people doing in the photos?
   2 What are they wearing? Describe the costumes.

3 Read this text about the Notting Hill Carnival. Then watch the film and find another seven mistakes.

> The Notting Hill Carnival is a huge
> London carnival – about a ~~thousand~~ *million*
> people come to be in the carnival or to watch
> it. It happens every July. There are about
> 17 bands with their own music, costumes
> and carnival queen. The costumes are very
> important for the carnival.
>
> Clary Salandy started designing costumes
> 50 years ago. Her carnival queen is a young
> woman called Tamiko, who doesn't have a
> lot of experience. She puts on her carnival
> costume – it's very uncomfortable because
> it's very heavy. When it comes to the carnival
> weekend, the bands parade through the
> streets – the costumes look amazing and it's
> a boring experience.

4 Discuss.
   1 Did you enjoy the film about the Notting Hill Carnival? Why/Why not?
   2 Do you have a big carnival in your town/country? What does it celebrate?
   3 What kind of things do people do at carnivals in your country?

1 Discuss.

1 Look at the painting by Richard Tate. Do you know which city it is? How do you know?

2 Do you like the painting?

3 How do you think Richard Tate made this painting?

    a He painted it from his head.

    b He sat in front of the buildings and painted it.

    c He painted it from a photo.

4 Why do you think Richard paints scenes from the city?

2 Look at the photos of buildings from London. Do you know any of these buildings?

3 Watch the film. Do you see the buildings from Exercise 2 in Richard's paintings (in the film), just in the film, or both? Tick the correct boxes. Watch carefully!

	photo	painting
a St Paul's Cathedral	☐	☐
b Battersea Power Station	☐	☐
c Tower Bridge	☐	☐
d The Dome	☐	☐
e The London Eye	☐	☐

4 Discuss.

1 Did you enjoy this film? Why/Why not?

2 Do you think that it gives a good impression of London?

3 Richard takes photos of London to do his paintings. Do you take photos? What kind of photos do you take?

1 Discuss.

1 What are the people in the photos doing?

2 How many ways of getting to work can you see in the photos? What are they?

3 Can you think of any other ways of getting to work?

2 Match the words and phrases with the meanings.

1	motorway	a	get up late
2	pick up	b	not working
3	space	c	collect someone or something from a place
4	company	d	types of train
5	oversleep	e	a big fast road
6	cancelled	f	at the correct time
7	tube/mainline	g	room to move around
8	on time	h	somebody to talk to

3 Watch the film and tick (✓) the correct column(s).

		Penelope	Jonathan	Liz	Mike	Johnny and Rachel
1	walk to the station	☐	☐	☐	☐	☐
2	cycle to the office	☐	☐	☐	☐	☐
3	drive along the motorway	☐	☐	☐	☐	☐
4	have breakfast on the train	☐	☐	☐	☐	☐
5	read a book/a newspaper	☐	☐	☐	☐	☐
6	listen to the radio	☐	☐	☐	☐	☐
7	think public transport is noisy	☐	☐	☐	☐	☐
8	like short journeys	☐	☐	☐	☐	☐
9	usually on time	☐	☐	☐	☐	☐
10	never late	☐	☐	☐	☐	☐
11	sometimes late	☐	☐	☐	☐	☐

4 Discuss.

1 Did you think the film was interesting?

2 Who do you think has the easiest/most difficult journey to work?

3 Is your journey to work the same or different from the ones in the extract? How?

4 Do you agree with the opinions about the advantages and disadvantages of commuting?

A   B   C

1 Look at the activities in the photographs and discuss these questions.

  1 Have you learnt the skills in the photos?

  2 Have you learnt any other physical skills? Which one(s)?

  3 Is learning a physical skill different from learning academic subjects? Why?

  4 The film is about rock climbing. Have you ever been rock climbing? Did you enjoy it?

2 Match the words and phrases on the left with their meanings on the right.

1	a challenge	a	safe
2	take up (an activity)	b	when you want to try new things
3	spirit of adventure	c	a difficult task or activity
4	secure	d	go up or down very quickly, e.g. a hill
5	steep	e	when you haven't done a lot (of an activity)
6	inexperienced	f	start doing (an activity)

3 Match the pictures with the labels. Then watch the film extract and check.

1 rock boots	2 a helmet	3 a knot
4 a rope	5 a harness	

4 Are these statements true (T) or false (F)? Correct the false ones.

  1 Marian and Andy have done a lot of climbing. ☐

  2 Climbers don't have to use a lot of equipment. ☐

  3 Marian was scared at first when she started the climb. ☐

  4 Marian leads the way when they start climbing. ☐

  5 Stuart teaches Marian and Andy to make secure knots. ☐

  6 Andy says he doesn't want to climb again. ☐

5 Discuss.

  1 Did you enjoy the extract? Do you want to try rock climbing now? Why/Why not?

  2 Have you done any physical activities like rock climbing? What?

  3 Do you prefer physical or mental challenges? Why?

1 _____

2 _____

3 _____

4 _____

5 _____

6 _____

1 Discuss.

   1 What do you usually do on holiday?
   2 Do you think everyday holidays are interesting or not?
   3 Would you like to do something different on holiday? What?

2 Write labels for photos 1–6. Use some of the activities a–j in the list in Exercise 3.

3 Look at this list of activities. With a partner write 1–10 in the YOU column.
   1 is your favourite.

		YOU	GILL	
a	bungee jumping	☐	☐	It's _____.
b	swimming with dolphins	☐	☐	Dolphins are _____.
c	whale watching	☐	☐	Where? _____
d	an expedition to Antarctica	☐	☐	It's _____ to get there.
e	diving	☐	☐	It's _____.
f	skiing	☐	☐	Where? _____
g	dog sledging	☐	☐	Where? _____
h	sailing a ship	☐	☐	What type of ship? _____
i	parascending	☐	☐	It's the closest thing to _____.
j	riding the rapids	☐	☐	It's _____!

4 Now watch the film and complete the GILL column. 1 is Gills favourite. Answer the
   questions or complete the notes with one or two words.

5 Discuss.

   1 Did you agree with Gill's list? Why/Why not?
   2 Compare your own 'top 10 adventures' with other students.

Writing Bank

Part 1 | Types of writing

1 Emails

- *Email* means 'electronic mail'.
- Emails can be formal or informal.
- We don't include addresses or dates in the text of emails.
- Informal emails often begin with *Hi* + name, not *Dear* + name. (the greeting)
- In the opening sentence we usually thank the recipient (the person we are writing to) for their last email (or phone call/ letter, etc.).
- In the closing sentence we usually mention a future plan or wish (e.g. *I hope you can come./ Write soon.*).
- At the end of an email to a friend or colleague we write *Best wishes,* + name. For a close friend or family member we can write *Love,* + name.

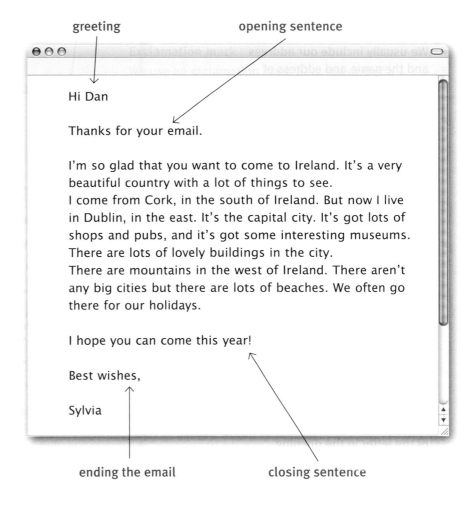

greeting   opening sentence

Hi Dan

Thanks for your email.

I'm so glad that you want to come to Ireland. It's a very beautiful country with a lot of things to see.
I come from Cork, in the south of Ireland. But now I live in Dublin, in the east. It's the capital city. It's got lots of shops and pubs, and it's got some interesting museums. There are lots of lovely buildings in the city.
There are mountains in the west of Ireland. There aren't any big cities but there are lots of beaches. We often go there for our holidays.

I hope you can come this year!

Best wishes,

Sylvia

ending the email   closing sentence

2 Postcards

- Postcards are usually informal.
- We often send postcards when we are on holiday, or to thank people for invitations, parties, etc.
- We don't include our address in postcards.
- We begin postcards with *Dear* + name. (the greeting)
- In the closing sentence we usually mention a wish or a future plan (e.g. *See you soon*).
- We often write *Love,* + name at the end.

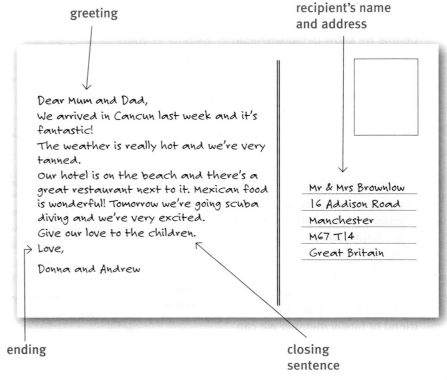

greeting   recipient's name and address

Dear Mum and Dad,
We arrived in Cancun last week and it's fantastic!
The weather is really hot and we're very tanned.
Our hotel is on the beach and there's a great restaurant next to it. Mexican food is wonderful! Tomorrow we're going scuba diving and we're very excited.
Give our love to the children.
Love,

Donna and Andrew

Mr & Mrs Brownlow
16 Addison Road
Manchester
M67 T14
Great Britain

ending   closing sentence

143

Female 2: I think the new shopping centre in Bath's got a good restaurant.

Female 1: Well, let's go to the shopping centre in the morning and then we can have lunch there.

Female 2: OK, that sounds good.

Male: Let's meet at eleven and we can get the bus.

Female 1: OK. We'll meet at eleven outside the bus station.

Unit 10. Journeys

Recording 10.1

Jason: I'm here at Heathrow Airport with the Garfield family: Derek and Moira and their children Todd and Alicia. Today's the start of an amazing adventure for them. In half an hour they get on a plane to begin the holiday of a lifetime. Derek, how are you feeling right now?

Derek: To be honest, Jason, I'm feeling quite nervous ... nervous but excited.

Jason: Why are you nervous?

Derek: Well, this is my first long plane journey. I've never been on a long-haul flight before so it's my first time ... and Australia is a long way away.

Jason: Are the rest of you experienced travellers?

Alicia: We've been to America!

Moira: Yes, the three of us have been on a long-haul flight before. I took Todd and Alicia to Florida last year.

Jason: Have you ever been to Australia?

Moira: No, we haven't.

Derek, Alicia, Todd: No, we've never been to Australia.

Jason: So I guess you are all very excited about those activities in Australia? Have you ever been horse-riding, hiking or bungee jumping before?

Todd: Alicia and I have been horse-riding. We went horse-riding when we were in Scotland two years ago. But mum and dad stayed in the hotel! They've never been on a horse!

Moira: It was cold!

Derek: But we've all been hiking. We went last year.

Jason: And have you ever been bungee jumping?

Derek: Oh no. We haven't been bungee jumping. It's the first time for all of us.

Moira: I'm very nervous about it!

Recording 10.2

1 But have you ever <u>been</u> to Australia?
2 No, we've never <u>been</u> there.

Recording 10.3

1 Have you been to the cinema in Italy?
2 I've never been on a ship with him.
3 Has she ever been to dinner in Finland?
4 We've never been to Paris in spring.

Recording 10.4

parked, seen, bought, had, written, got

Recording 10.5

1 have 2 fit 3 short 4 park 5 bald 6 sleep

Recording 10.6

Julia: The way I commute to work is probably quite unusual! I rollerblade! I live in Surfside, a suburb in the north of Miami and I work at a hotel on Miami beach. It takes about twenty-five minutes to get to work. And of course it costs nothing. It's usually warm and sunny in Miami and rollerblading is very healthy – I really enjoy it. But rollerblading is a bit dangerous when you cross busy roads. And it's tiring!

Billy: Commuting is really difficult in London. It's a huge city and there's a lot of traffic. You can't really commute by car because it's impossible to park in the centre of London. There's a good underground system but there aren't any stations near my house so I get the bus to work. It isn't expensive but it's sometimes quite slow because of all the traffic. And I hate waiting at the bus stop in the winter, it's very boring!

Recording 10.7

Agent: Good morning. Distant Dreams Travel.

Billy: Oh, hello. Do you sell airline tickets for New Zealand?

Agent: Yes.

Billy: Right. I'd like four tickets from London Heathrow to New Zealand.

Agent: What's your exact destination?

Billy: Auckland.

Agent: And when do you want to go?

Billy: I'd like to go on Friday the fifth of next month.

Agent: Return or one-way?

Billy: I'd like return tickets, please. We want to come back one month later.

Agent: OK. I'll just check on the computer. OK, do you want economy or business class?

Billy: Oh, business class is expensive. I prefer economy. How much is that?

Agent: Let me see. Four return tickets in economy, and your departure date is the fifth. OK. We've got Air New Zealand and Qantas for those dates. On Air New Zealand it's six thousand New Zealand dollars, about two thousand pounds. Qantas is more expensive – about two thousand, three hundred pounds, but it's a shorter flight. Which do you prefer?

Billy: The cheaper one, Air New Zealand, I think. What time does the flight leave London?

Agent: At ten thirty in the morning.

Billy: Is it a direct flight?

Agent: No, there's a short stop in Bangkok.

Billy: Fine. I'd like four tickets then, please.

Recording 10.8

Reception: Hello. Hotel Europa. Can I help you?

Woman: Yes. I'd like to book a room, please.

Reception: OK. For how many nights?

Woman: For two nights.

Reception: Which dates, please.

Woman: For the 15th and 16th of May, please.

Reception: OK, that's fine. Would you like a single or double room?

Woman: Do you have twin rooms?

Reception: Yes, we do.

Woman: I'd like to book a twin room, then. Does it have a private bathroom?

Reception: All our rooms have private bathrooms, madam.

Woman: Oh, OK. How much is that, please?

Reception: That's 240 euros, 120 a night.

Woman: Is breakfast included?

Reception: No, it isn't. Breakfast is ten euros.

Woman: OK. Oh, just one thing. Can I book a beauty treatment before we come?

Reception: Yes, madam. I can transfer you to the beauty salon, but can I take your name and credit card details first, please?

Recording 10.9

1

Reception: Can I help you, madam?

Woman: Yes. I asked for a twin room.

Reception: Yes, madam.

Woman: Well, you've given me a double room.

Reception: Oh, I am sorry, madam.

Woman: Can we have a twin room, please?

Reception: I'll just have a look ... yes, we have one on the second floor.

2

Reception: Reception. Can I help you?

Man: Yes, I asked for tea with my breakfast.

Reception: Yes?

Man: And you've given me coffee.

Reception: I'm sorry, sir. I'll call the kitchen and get you some tea.

Man: OK. Thank you.

3

Reception: Yes, sir, can I help you?

Man: Yes, I booked golf for this morning.

Reception: Yes, sir?

Man: The golf club has just told me that there isn't a booking for me.

Reception: Oh, that's strange. I'm sure the golf club can fit you in later. I'll call them and sort it out for you.

Unit 11. Learning

Recording 11.1

Biology, Chemistry, college, Geography, History, kindergarten, Languages,

Mathematics, Physics, polytechnic, primary school, Science, secondary school, university

Recording 11.2

Part 1

Welcome to the free Tourist Information Line for visitors to Great Britain. For information on visas and immigration, please press one. For information on driving in Britain, please press two. For information on hotels, please press three. For information on public transport in Britain, please press four. To return to this menu at any time press the star key. You have chosen option two: driving in Britain.

Part 2

If you have a valid driving licence from your own country, you can drive in Britain without a British licence for six months. After six months, you have to get a British driving licence. To get a British licence you have to take a driving test. You can find information about the British driving test on our website.

To rent a car in Britain you have to have a valid driving licence from your country and a credit card. Drivers under the age of 18 can't rent cars in Britain.

When you are driving in Britain, you don't have to keep your documents with you. The British drive on the left side of the road and, unlike the United States, you can't turn right at a red traffic light. For more information on British driving regulations, please look at our website. That is the end of the driving section. To return to the main menu press the star key.

Recording 11.3

You don't have to be a British citizen to take a British driving test but you have to have a valid British visa.

Recording 11.4

1 leaf 2 few 3 fan 4 v

Recording 11.5

1 Philip finds French films very violent.
2 Very few fines feel fair.
3 Fiona Philips never gives fitness advice to fresh fruit fanatics.

Recording 11.6

Steve:

We don't have a lot of rules in the United States really. I mean we don't have to do military service and we don't have to have identity cards. You can drive when you're 16 and you can even buy a gun when you're 21!

But some things aren't so easy. You have to be 21 to go into a bar or a nightclub, and smoking is difficult – you can't smoke in offices, shops or restaurants. And of course we have to pay when we see a doctor or go to hospital.

Recording 11.7

Interviewer: Nicole, tell us about the educational system in New Zealand. For example, how long do students spend in the system?

Nicole: Oh, ... a long time! Usually about 17 or 18 years if they go to university.

Interviewer: When did you start school?

Nicole: At the age of five. Compulsory education is twelve years – from five to about sixteen, but a lot of children in New Zealand go to pre-school classes, you know, kindergartens. I went to a kindergarten when I was four and after a year I went to primary school.

Interviewer: How many years were you at primary school?

Nicole: Five years – from five to ten.

Interviewer: Where did you go after primary school?

Nicole: Well, then I went to an intermediate school, from ten to twelve. Then at twelve we start at secondary school.

Interviewer: Mmm. When can students leave secondary school?

Nicole: Well, we can leave secondary school at sixteen, but most students stay till they're eighteen.

Interviewer: Do a lot of students go on to higher education?

Nicole: Yes, I think about fifty per cent of students go into higher education – that's universities, polytechnics, colleges of education ...

Interviewer: Which type of institution did you go to?

Nicole: I went to a college of education because I wanted to be a teacher. I became a primary teacher, so I studied for three years and finished when I was twenty-two.

Interviewer: Do you have to pay for your higher education studies in New Zealand?

Nicole: Yes, we have to pay some of the costs, but not all.

Interviewer: How much does a student have to pay?

Nicole: Oh, it depends. It can be 2,000 dollars or it can be 20,000.

Interviewer: Well, thank you, Nicole. That was very interesting ...

Recording 11.8

1 What did you do there?
2 Was it interesting?
3 Who did you see? 4 Did you like it?

Recording 11.9

1 How does the educational system work?
2 How long do students spend in the system?
3 When did you start school?
4 How many years were you at primary school?
5 What subjects did you take?
6 Where did you go after primary school?
7 Which type of institution did you go to?
8 How much does a student have to pay?

Recording 11.10

Host: Good afternoon. Welcome to Live to Learn. People today often want to continue learning through their lives, but what are their choices? First, let's talk to Aileen Murphy, head of Haresfield Adult College.

Local College: Good afternoon. Well, at Haresfield College, we organise classes in local schools and in our centre. The classes are usually in the evening, but we do have some day classes. Most of our classes are once a week, for about three hours.

H: What can you study at your college?

LC: Well, we have classes in academic subjects, such as History. We offer five foreign languages and we also offer courses in vocational subjects like Computing.

H: How much do the courses cost?

LC: An average course costs about £100 for an academic year.

H: Thank you, Aileen. Now we have Graham Knight, from the Open University.

OU: Well, the Open University is a distance-learning university – that is, you study at home. There are a few classes during the year, and there are often summer schools. Our students have to study for about 12 hours a week.

H: Thank you, Graham. Oh, what about cost?

OU: Most of our courses are about £500 a year, at the moment.

H: Thanks. Now, Beth Anderson works for a professional training company, MicroMatters Ltd.

MM: Right. We offer training courses in computer skills for people who are actually working with computers.

H: Do you offer courses to people who aren't working?

MM: Oh, yes. Most of our courses last two or three days, for people in work, but we also have week-long courses and evening courses.

H: And the cost?

MM: A week's course costs about £900. Of course, we provide everything – the trainers, the training room, the computers – the trainees don't have to pay for any extras, so we aren't cheap.

H: Thank you. Now, finally, James Beecham, to tell us about the University of the Third Age.

U3A: Good afternoon. The University of the Third Age is for retired people, so it is mostly older people. We have groups across the country, and each group organises its own courses. Usually, the group uses a hall in its town, or a local school, and lecturers come to speak to the group. We try to make our type of learning very cheap. Members have to pay £2.50 to join, and then a small part of the costs – so it is very cheap.

H: Yes, I see. And what kind of courses or subjects do you offer?

U3A: Well, the speakers talk about their special subjects or their interests, so we have a lot of different topics, but it's not usually very academic.

H: Right. Thank you, everyone, for coming. Now, let's move on to …

Recording 11.11

Man: Hello. Staff room.

Carlos: Hello. Can I speak to Mrs Alders, please?

Man: Just a moment. I'll get her. Jill, it's for you.

Alders: Hello. Jill Alders.

Carlos: Mrs Alders? It's Carlos Brent. My son, Karl, is in your class.

Alders: Oh yes, Mr Brent. How can I help you?

Carlos: I'd like to meet you next week to talk about Karl's examinations.

Alders: Fine. Can you come on Thursday? I'm teaching in the morning but I'm free in the afternoon.

Carlos: I'm afraid I can't come then because I'm working. What about Wednesday?

Alders: No, I'm afraid I'm teaching all day on Wednesday.

Carlos: Well, I can come on Tuesday.

Alders: Er, Tuesday. Well, I'm teaching a class at ten thirty and I'm taking the children swimming in the afternoon.

Carlos: How about earlier in the morning?

Alders: Let me see … OK. Let's meet at nine o'clock.

Carlos: Nine o'clock on Tuesday morning. Thank you very much.

Alders: I'll see you next week then. You can come to the staff room …

Unit 12. Ambitions

Recording 12.1

Dario: Look, here's the photo of us rafting on the Colorado River last summer.

Mia: Oh yes. That was so frightening. I didn't really enjoy that – the raft went so fast! It was really dangerous.

Dario: Well, I thought it was fantastic.

Mia: I preferred trekking in the Grand Canyon really.

Dario: Yes, that was fun. But a bit slow. And do you remember when we went on those bikes in the hills behind San Francisco?

Mia: Yes. I remember cycling up the hills and through all those tunnels!

Dario: Yes, that was great.

Mia: Mm, I really enjoyed that. Do you think that was the best part of our trip?

Dario: No, horse-riding was the best. That was really exciting.

Mia: Yeah, You're right. I think horse-riding was my favourite too. It was a lot of fun.

Recording 12.2

I'm going to stop smoking.

Recording 12.3

1 She's going to lose weight.
2 They're going to sell their car.
3 We're going to learn French.
4 I'm going to buy a laptop.

Recording 12.4

Song: Fame!

Baby look at me
And tell me what you see
You ain't seen the best of me yet
Give me time and I'll make you forget the rest
I've got more in me
And you can set it free
I can catch the moon in my hand
Don't you know who I am?
Remember my name

Chorus
Fame!
I'm gonna live forever
I'm gonna learn how to fly
Fame! I feel it coming together
People will see me and cry
Fame! I'm gonna make it to heaven
Light up the sky like a flame
Fame! I'm gonna live forever
Baby, remember my name!

Recording 12.5

1 Victoria

I've joined the drama group at university because I really love performing. I'm going to learn how to sing and dance. I want to act in plays and musicals and of course I'd like to be famous one day. Sometimes TV producers watch our student shows so anything is possible!

2 Helena

My ambition is to become a famous politician, perhaps a minister in the government. At the moment I'm just a student – I'm studying politics at college. But I'm going to work for a politician next summer. I want to learn more about elections and voting. I'm really excited about it.

3 Lewis

I've just had my first training session with the team, so I'm a bit tired. It's only the reserve team but I'm going to practise with them twice a week to improve my physical fitness and ball control skills. I'm going to work really hard to get into the first team. I know I'm a good footballer and I'm sure I'm good enough to get a place in a professional team. These days footballers are the biggest stars in the world, and I'd really like to be rich and famous.

Recording 12.6

Andi: Good morning. Charity Challenge, Andi speaking. How can I help you?

David: Oh, hello. My name's David MacMahon. I'm interested in doing one of your challenges and I'd like to ask some questions.

Andi: That's fine, David. Please, go ahead.

David: Well, first, where exactly do the challenges take place?

Andi: All over the world, in Africa, Latin America, and the Caribbean, Asia, the Middle East and Europe.

David: Oh, I see. And what kind of challenges are they? I mean, what kind of activities are they?

Andi: Well, we have hiking, cycling, sailing, rafting, mountain climbing and horse-riding.

David: Oh good. I enjoy hiking and I love cycling – I use my bike every day – but I hate horse-riding and I don't like sailing.

Andi: What about rafting and mountain climbing?

David: I wouldn't like to climb a mountain, and I've never done any rafting, but I'd like to try. Do you have to be very fit?

Andi: Yes, you do. Our expeditions are difficult and you have to have a good level of fitness. Choose an activity you know you can do, start training very early and join a gym.

David: Oh, I can't stand going to the gym … it's so boring, but I can train in other ways.

Andi: Yes, and we have training weekends. People find them very useful.

David: Yes, I think I'd like to do a training weekend. How often do you have them?

Andi: About once a month.

David: OK. Who pays for the expedition?

Andi: Well, you pay for the expedition. We also ask you to raise money for your charity.

David: Oh, yes, of course. Who chooses the charity?

Andi: You choose the charity. Do you have any other questions, David?

David: Yes, just one. How do I raise the money?

Andi: We can help you with ideas. For example, you could do a car boot sale to get money.

David: Oh, I'd like to do that. I love going to car boot sales, but I've never done one.

Andi: OK. So do you want to join one of our expeditions, David?

David: I want to think about it for a few days. I'd like to find out more. Can you send me some information?

Andi: Certainly. I can send you a brochure and …

Recording 12.7

I'd really like to play the classical guitar.

Recording 12.8

1 white 2 Dave 3 late 4 mine 5 lake

Recording 12.9

1 I hate waiting for bus rides in the rain.
2 Mike likes riding his bike but he hates playing games.
3 We prefer safe day trains to late night flights.